The Alamo

The Alamo

AN ILLUSTRATED HISTORY

Edwin P. Hoyt

Taylor Publishing Company
Dallas, Texas

Designed by David Timmons

Published by Taylor Publishing Company
1550 West Mockingbird Lane
Dallas, Texas 75235
www.taylorpub.com

Library of Congress Cataloging-in-Publication Data:

Hoyt. Edwin Palmer.
    The Alamo : an illustrated history / Edwin P. Hoyt.
        p.   cm.
    Includes bibliographical references (p. 182) and index.
    ISBN 087833-204-9
        1. Alamo (San Antonio, Tex.)—Siege, 1836—Pictorial works. 2. Alamo (San Antonio, Tex.)—History—Pictorial works. 3. San Antonio (Tex.)—History—Pictorial works. I. Title.
F390.H915 1999
976.4′351—dc21   99-10697
                                                    CIP

10   9   8   7   6   5   4   3   2   1
Printed in the United States of America

p. ii: The restored Alamo as it appears today, maintained by the Daughters of the Republic of Texas. *Texas State Library & Archives Commission*

To the memory of those heroes who fell at the Alamo, with the reminder that they were both Texians and Tejanos.

Contents

Preface

The Alamo.

The very name conjures visions of blood, sweat, and tears. Smells, sights, and sounds: the acrid stink of gunpowder, the gleaming steel of bayonets, the screams of frightened horses, the shouts of soldiers as they move to attack, the booming of cannon, and the popping of rifles and muskets. The cries of the wounded, and the awful silence of the dead.

It was not a big battle or even a very important one. When it was over and the last defender had fallen, General Santa Anna, the victor, felt great relief that one obstacle to rebellion's elimination had been removed.

But within hours, the news of the Battle of the Alamo had begun to spread across Texas, and men by the hundreds rallied to the rebel cause.

"Remember the Alamo!" was their war cry, and it shook the world.

Texas People

Texan	Person who lives in Texas; more specifically, person born in Texas
Texian	Texas colonist, usually but not exclusively from the United States
Tejano	Person of Mexican origin who lives in Texas
Norteamericano	Spanish term for an American colonist in Texas

INTRODUCTION

The Alamo

The orders were clear. (Later, Col. James Bowie would say they were discretionary.) He was to take a detachment of more than thirty men to San Antonio de Béxar. There he would meet Lt. Col. James Clinton Neill, commander of the Texian garrison, and decide what was to be done with the Alamo, the old mission that had been turned into a fortress. The Texian War of Independence had broken out in the autumn of 1835 and the Texians had captured San Antonio in December. After that easy victory the volunteers of the victorious army had decided that the war was won, and their army had disintegrated. Now in January 1836, Colonel Neill had only eighty men to defend San Antonio against the attack he soon expected to be launched by the Mexican Army.

On January 17, 1836, Gen. Sam Houston wrote Gov. Henry Smith from Goliad:

> Colonel Bowie will leave here within a few hours for Bexar, with a detachment of from thirty to fifty men.... I have ordered the fortifications in the town of Bexar to be demolished, and if you should think well of it, I will remove all the cannon and other munitions of war to Gonzales and Copano, blow up the Alamo, and abandon the place, as it will be impossible to keep up the Station with volunteers. The sooner I can be authorized the better it will be for the country.

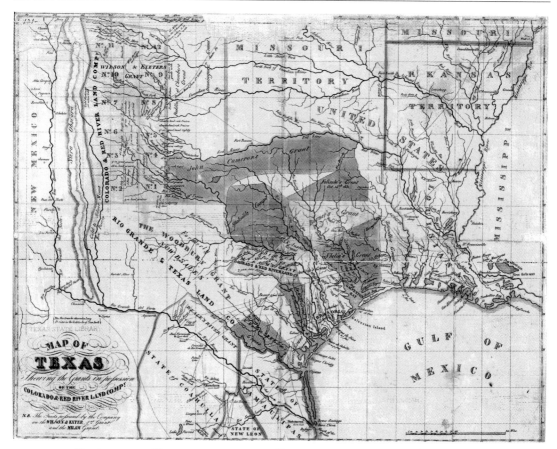

THIS MAP OF TEXAS PRIOR TO THE TEXAS WAR OF INDEPENDENCE SHOWS LAND
GRANTS IN POSSESSION OF THE COLORADO AND RED LAND COMPANY. IN ADDI-
TION TO TEXAS, LOUISIANA, THE ARKANSAS TERRITORY, AND PARTS OF THE
MISSOURI TERRITORY, IT DESCRIBES THE MEXICAN STATES OF COAHUILA AND
TAMAULIPAS.
TEXAS STATE LIBRARY & ARCHIVES COMMISSION

He called Colonel Bowie in and explained his strategy for the war against
the Mexicans: The Mexican Army was modeled on Napoleonic lines and the
Texians could not hope to equal their cavalry, which could sweep through level
ground like a scythe. But Mexico's center of government was south and west, a
long way from Texas, and as the campaign continued, their supply lines would
grow longer and more brittle. General Houston's plan was to wear down the
enemy by raids and forays, avoiding confrontation, and finally to draw them
into battle in the forest country of East Texas, where the rifles of the Texians
would be at best advantage.

"For the moment," General Houston said, "we have to fight a defensive
war." He told him what he had written to Col. James Fannin earlier. Houston
knew that everything that had happened—Gonzales, Goliad, Concepción, San

IN THE YEARS PRIOR TO THE CIVIL WAR, THE ALAMO WAS RESTORED AND USED
BY THE U.S. ARMY QUARTERMASTER CORPS AS A SUPPLY DEPOT.
*THE SAN ANTONIO LIGHT COLLECTION, UT INSTITUTE OF TEXAN CULTURES AT
SAN ANTONIO*

Antonio—was just good luck. The Mexicans had just begun to
fight. Gov. Henry Smith called the ragtag Texian army "a
mob nicknamed an army"—and he was about right. They
desperately needed artillery, but it wouldn't arrive from
New Orleans until March. They had no tents, arms,
ammunition, or food to keep any kind of real force
in the field. Houston's idea was to keep only
enough troops to man the defenses at Goliad and
Gonzales and to furlough all the others.

Houston had recently received a letter from
Green Jameson, chief engineer of the Alamo,
describing the fortress. That
description had convinced
the general that the Alamo
was not defensible. The dilap-
idated Spanish mission was
not the place to make a stand.

SAM HOUSTON AS
HE APPEARED IN
THE LATE 1830S.
*CENTER FOR
AMERICAN HISTORY,
UNIVERSITY OF TEXAS
AT AUSTIN*

The man he was sending to the Alamo was no stranger to San Antonio. In fact San Antonio was Colonel Bowie's home. He had come to Texas in 1828 at the age of thirty-three, a tall, handsome man who was already a living legend, known as the greatest fighter in the West. He met and captivated the governor, Don Juan Martín Veramendi, and married his eldest daughter, Ursula. He arrived in San Antonio famous for the knife that was his brother's invention, the big blade with which he had fought many duels. He had taken a house in the Calle Soledad, a few doors from the governor's palace, and gone into business with the governor. He had become a Mexican citizen and converted to the Church of Rome. He had also become active in local affairs, and had raised a military company of young aristocrats who elected him colonel.

It had been an idyllic existence, one distanced from his previous life as slave trader and land speculator by time and Texas. He had settled down and become an ideal citizen. In 1832 he had played a prominent role in the Nacogdoches Incident, in which the *norteamericanos* declared their support for General Santa Anna and the Constitution of 1824 against *Presidente* Anastasio Bustamante, who controlled the local authorities.

That had marked Bowie's entrance into the struggle for Texian rights. Then, in 1833, Bowie went east on a business trip. While he was gone, his entire family, including Ursula and the governor, were carried off in a cholera epidemic. From that point on, the grieving Bowie devoted his life to the cause of Texas. Now he was a colonel with the Texas Volunteers, and the one man General Houston trusted above all others to carry out his orders.

It was not just that they were the same kind of people, although that was certainly true. Both Bowie and Houston were hard-drinking, fearless fighting men who had tilted a jug together innumerable times when the Texian Council was meeting in San Felipe de Austin to decide the fate of Texas.

Houston had come to trust Jim Bowie. The Louisiana brawler was cool under fire, and always did what he was ordered to do. In this land of individuals, that was a rare quality. Sam Houston had been let down half a dozen times by men he had trusted, but never by Jim Bowie. He expected Bowie to follow his orders.

On January 17, Colonel Bowie led his company of volunteers out of Goliad. In his jacket was a letter from Houston to Neill urging him to demolish the Alamo and pull back to Gonzales and Copano. He was accompanied by Col. James Bonham, commander of the Mobile Greys, a force raised in the American state of Alabama to fight the Texians' war. After they left Goliad, General Houston then turned his attention to another pressing matter, an incipient rebellion against his authority.

Dr. James Grant, a doctor turned speculator who had interests in Mexico, proposed to lead an expedition to attack Matamoros, a city of 12,000 on the other side of the Rio Grande. General Houston had first favored the idea, but then turned against it as too risky. A few hundred men were not enough for the job, and Dr. Grant had begun to challenge Houston's authority.

Clothed with the authority of the Texas Legislative Council, early in January 1836 Dr. Grant had stripped the Alamo and the Goliad garrisons of ammunition and supplies, and was taking his men twenty-five miles southeast to the town of Refugio. There they would jump off for Matamoros. Half the New Orleans Greys had joined the Matamoros Expedition. Grant was calling himself commander in chief of the expedition. Houston was too wise to challenge just then, but he rode along with the column and joked and chatted with the men like the Tennessee politician he had been in the past. Casually he let it be known to the soldiers that this was a fool's expedition. His manner was so casual that it was convincing. The men began to have their doubts.

By the time they reached Refugio those doubts had become serious. But at Refugio, Houston encountered another crisis, one which showed how close to disintegration the Texians' bid for freedom had come.

At Refugio, Dr. Grant's column was joined by Col. Francis W. Johnson, who also laid claim to leadership of the Matamoros Expedition, and some more men.

Johnson had stunning news: The Texas Council had ousted Gov. Henry Smith, deposed General Houston as commander in chief of the army, and authorized still another man, Col. James Fannin, to lead the Matamoros Expedition.

Houston decided he must go immediately to Washington-on-the-Brazos, the temporary capital of Texas, to learn the news at first hand. But before he left

Refugio, Houston called the men together and gave them a speech. One source recounts his words like this:

> Before you set out on this expedition I just want to remind you of a few facts. How do you think a handful of men who have marched twenty-two days without breadstuffs are going to capture a town of 12,000 people?
>
> And remember that the Mexicans will regard you as mercenaries and treat you accordingly. In war when spoil is the object, friends and enemies share one common destiny.

Then Houston rode off, leaving a growing number of bewildered soldiers behind him.

General Houston arrived at the capital to report to Governor Smith, who assured him that he, Smith, was still governor, and Houston was still commander in chief. Houston wanted to resign, but Smith talked him out of it. He persuaded Houston to visit the Cherokees and prevent an uprising while the Texians were fighting the Mexicans. Houston had lived with the Cherokees, and was an honorary member of the Cherokee nation. With the governor's blessing, he prepared to set off for the camp of his old friend Chief Bowles, to work out a new treaty.

By the time he got back, the governor said, things should have settled down.

Colonel Bowie and his company arrived at San Antonio on January 19 and were greeted by Colonel Neill. Bowie handed Neill the orders from General Houston and Neill told him his woes. The garrison was decreasing just about every day. The soldiers had not been paid for months—who could blame them for wandering off? There were no horses for scouting, no powder or balls for the cannon, no medical supplies. The crowd bound for Matamoros had even stripped the garrison of their clothing. There had been some reinforcements. The New Orleans Greys had come in their neat gray uniforms, but half of them had left with Dr. Grant and the rest were not real soldiers. They refused to drill, they had taken up residence in the ruins of the Alamo chapel and did as they pleased.

Still, when Neill showed Bowie around the Alamo, Bowie was impressed with the improvements the colonel had made since taking over. He had brought nineteen of the cannon captured from the Mexicans into the fort, including an eighteen-pounder. Green Jameson, the lawyer turned garrison engineer, had sited them on the fort walls. The place was beginning to look like a real fort. Maybe it could be successfully defended after all. Colonel Neill thought it could and his enthusiasm was infectious. Within days, Bowie decided against destroying the Alamo. Using his web of local contacts, he found food and horses. He visited Tejano friends and returned with intelligence about the Mexican Army. Gen. Antonio López de Santa Anna, the president of Mexico, had been reported marching from the west with 4,600 men.

Supplies began to arrive from Bowie's friends: beeves, corn, ammunition for the cannon. On January 26, Bowie attended a mass meeting which ended with a declaration from the soldiers that they

SKETCH OF WILLIAM BARRET TRAVIS BY WILEY MARTIN, DECEMBER 1835. THIS APPEARS IN THE BOOK, *MARGARET BALLENTINE*. DEGOLYER LIBRARY, SOUTHERN METHODIST UNIVERSITY

could and would hold the Alamo. Bowie wrote a letter to Governor Smith saying that in spite of General Houston's orders to destroy the Alamo, he and Colonel Neill had decided that it would be defended: "Col. Neill and I are agreed that we will die in these ditches rather than surrender this place."

The governor was impressed. Neill had manned the first cannon the Texians had ever had, at Gonzales, and he was an experienced artillery officer. Bowie had won the Battle of Concepción. In Houston's absence the governor decided to send Lt. Col. William Barret Travis to raise a company and reinforce the San Antonio garrison.

Travis did not want to go. He wrote a letter to the governor:

> I am willing, nay anxious, to go to the defense of Bexar, and I have done everything in my power to equip the enlisted men and get them off. But sir, I am unwilling to risk my reputation...by going off into the enemy's country with such little means....

But orders were orders, and in the end he decided to go to San Antonio. Soon, Bowie had word that Travis was coming with thirty more men to swell the garrison.

On January 27, a messenger galloped into the Alamo with word about the Mexicans. Gen. Joaquin Ramírez y Sesma was on the Rio Grande, heading toward San Antonio. Three days later another courier came with word that behind Sesma were five thousand more Mexican troops led by General Santa Anna. The president of Mexico had decided to take personal control of the suppression of this *norteamericano* rebellion, the courier said. That day another messenger was sent galloping to San Felipe with a new plea for reinforcement.

The 150 men of the Alamo waited. They were eager to take on all comers.

ALONG WITH JIM BOWIE AND WILLIAM TRAVIS, DAVY CROCKETT WAS ONE OF THE MOST FAMOUS OF THE ALAMO DEFENDERS. THIS PAINTING IS BY CHARLES B. NORMANN.
TEXAS STATE LIBRARY & ARCHIVES COMMISSION

Timeline

1500s	Spanish come to Texas.
1693	Franciscans in Nacogdoches.
1741	First chapel in San Antonio.
1803	Louisiana Purchase.
1820	Moses Austin receives land grant to settle American families in Texas.
1821	Stephen Austin begins bringing in settlers.
1824	Mexican Republic Constitution of 1824.
1828	James Bowie moves to Texas.
1829	First Mexican revolution.
1830	Anti-American immigration law.
1831	William Barret Travis comes to Texas.
1832	June, first confrontation between American settlers and Mexican authority at Anahuac. August, Nacogdoches Incident. Santa Anna triumphs over Bustamante, plans to become dictator.
1833	Convention at San Felipe petitions for Texas statehood. Stephen Austin carries petition to Mexico City. Austin is jailed for a year and a half.

1835

September	Stephen Austin returns to Texas embittered. Consultation assembly meets, declares war. As the committee is meeting, Gen. Martín Perfecto de Cós with 500 troops lands at Copano and begins the march to San Antonio. Citizens of Gonzales refuse to give up cannon given them earlier for protection against Indians. On September 30 the commander of San Antonio sends troops to get it.
October 1	The Gonzales men fire on the Mexican troops, who retreat. The Battle of Gonzales is the first action of the Texas War of Independence.
October 3	In Mexico City the Congress strips the states of authority, thus creating Santa Anna's Centralist dictatorship.
October 9	General Cós arrives at San Antonio and takes command of garrison. He begins fortifying the Alamo mission.
October 10	Rebels capture Goliad.
October 28	The Battle of Concepción.

October 30	The Mexican National Congress authorizes war against the Texas rebels.
November	The Siege of San Antonio.
November 3	Delegates convene the Consultation and decide to declare independence and establish a provisional government.
November 12	Sam Houston is chosen commander in chief but without authority over San Antonio army.
November 15	Capt. William Barret Travis captures a herd of horses and mules.
November 26	The Grass Fight. Col. James Bowie leads a detachment in an attack on a Mexican pack train south of San Antonio. The Mexicans send troops. Bowie triumphs but finds the pack train is carrying fodder.
November 28	Santa Anna leaves Mexico City to direct the Mexican Army against the Texians.
December 5	Ben Milam leads volunteers in attack on San Antonio. On the third day Milam is killed.
December 9	The capture of San Antonio.
December 12	James Butler Bonham's Mobile Greys arrive in San Antonio.
December 31	Santa Anna assembles his army at San Luis Potosí.

1836

January 7	Santa Anna's army arrives at Saltillo.
January 19	Jim Bowie arrives at the Alamo and decides to defend it.
January	Davy Crockett arrives at Nacogdoches, joins militia.
February 3	Travis arrives at the Alamo.
February 4	Fannin lands at Copano, marches to Refugio.
February 8	Crockett and twelve riflemen arrive at the Alamo.
February 11	Colonel Neill leaves the Alamo on leave; command is split between Bowie and Travis.
February 21	The siege of the Alamo begins.
February 23	Santa Anna arrives at San Antonio.
February 24	Sick Jim Bowie takes to his bed, leaving Travis in sole command of the Alamo garrison.
February 28	The Battle of San Patricio.
March 2	The Battle of Agua Dulce.
March 6	The fall of the Alamo.
March 19–20	The Battle of Coleto Creek.
March 27	The Goliad Massacre.
March–April	The "Runaway Scrape."
April 21	The Battle of San Jacinto.

ONE

Texas

GTT—Gone to Texas.

Scrawled on the door of an abandoned cabin anywhere in the southeast United States in 1830, this meant that the occupants had succumbed to "Texas fever" and gone west.

They were lured by the promise of a paradise, for that is how Texas was painted. "No sturdy forest here for months defies the axe," said the newspaper advertisements, guidebooks, and handbills, "but smiling prairies invite the plough. Here no humble prices reduce the stimulus to labor, but the reward of industry is so ample as to furnish the greatest incentive."

By the thousands, families moved to Texas in 1830 and the years after that. In Tennessee, blacksmith Almeron Dickinson read an advertisement and told his wife to start packing. They were going to Texas. In New York City, Dr. Amos Pollard awoke one morning in 1834 and picked up his morning newspaper. There was an advertisement for land in Columbia, Texas. Dr. Pollard, whose New York practice was not doing very well, decided to go to Texas on the spur of the moment.

The wave of immigration had its beginnings in the first quarter of the nineteenth century, when Spain relaxed its restrictions and began inviting *norteamericanos* to settle in this part of their Mexican colony. Over the previous 300 years, Spain had not been very successful in colonizing this area.

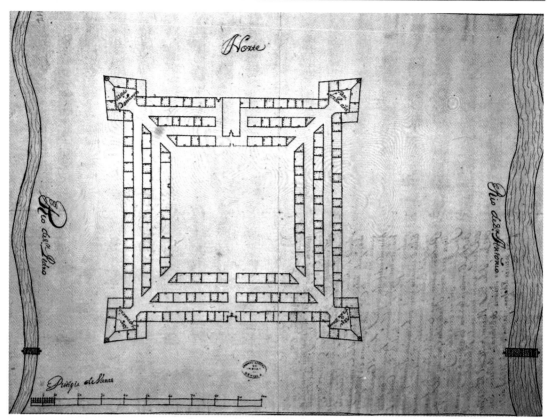

"PLANO DEL PRESIDIO DE SAN ANTONIO DE BÉXAR DE LA PROVINCIA DE TEXAS"
DESCRIBES THE FORTIFICATIONS AND BRIDGES AT THE PRESIDO OF BÉXAR AS
MAPPED OUT BY THE MARQUÉS DE SAN MIGEL DE AGUAYO.
TEXAS STATE LIBRARY & ARCHIVES COMMISSION

The first Spanish people came to Texas in the sixteenth century, bringing
Christianity and Castilian civilization across the Atlantic in a pattern typical of
Latin America. But in Texas the pattern did not work. When the Franciscans
appeared in 1693 at Nacogdoches to establish a mission, the mission never took
hold. A quarter of a century later they tried again, this time on the San Antonio
River. The *presidio* (garrison) established in this remote place was named after
the duke of Béxar—San Antonio de Béxar. In spite of these inauspicious beginnings, enough Spanish settlers appeared for a town to grow up around the *presidio*. Several villages in Spain's Canary Islands off the coast of Africa were co-
opted into settling in San Antonio.

By 1741, the first chapel was being built. In all, five missions would be built
in San Antonio. It became the hub of Spanish civilization in Texas. But the mission did not become the center of local life as it did, for example, in California.
The reason given by the authorities for failure—trouble with the French along
the border—masked the reality: The Indians in this section of Mexico were

IN THE EIGHTEENTH CENTURY, THE SPANISH GOVERNMENT CO-OPTED A NUMBER
OF CANARY ISLAND VILLAGES TO SETTLE IN SAN ANTONIO DE BÉXAR. THIS
DRAWING, MADE BY JOSÉ CISNEROS, SHOWS A YOUNG CANARY ISLAND GIRL
WITH A SOLDIER OF THE ERA IN FRONT OF THE ALAMO.
UT INSTITUTE OF TEXAN CULTURES AT SAN ANTONIO

MOSES AUSTIN, PLANNER OF THE AUSTIN COLONY IN TEXAS,
WHICH HIS SON, STEPHEN F. AUSTIN, SETTLED.
TEXAS STATE LIBRARY & ARCHIVES COMMISSION

mostly Apache and Comanche, both fiercely indepen-
dent nations. By the end of the eighteenth century,
there were fewer than 5,000 people living in the three
Spanish centers of La Bahía, San Antonio, and
Nacogdoches, with more than half of them in San
Antonio.

In 1803, America bought the entire Louisiana
Territory from France. The land extended to the Canadian
border, and American eyes turned westward. Spanish
resistance to foreign exploitation began to weaken. The real
breakthrough came in 1820, the year that Moses Austin, a Missouri

Stephen F. Austin
1793=1836

"WAR IS OUR ONLY RECOURSE"

A slender, curly-haired bachelor, Stephen Austin was the first of the
empresarios who brought Americans to the Mexican state of
Coahuila y Texas, where he ultimately settled over 1,500 families. In America
he had been a newspaper editor, businessman, and judge before he became a
land speculator. His father, Moses Austin, was a Spanish citizen, and Stephen
became a Mexican citizen with the establishment of the Republic after the
Revolution of 1820.

Austin wanted his people to be good Mexican citizens and in the early
years he was the ideal immigrant, moderate and law-abiding. As an *empresario* in 1823 he organized the first company of Texas Rangers to protect his
settlers from Indian raids. He served in the Coahuila y Texas legislature and
was the leading force in the Peace Party, which opposed radical efforts to
break Texas away from Mexico. Although he held strong prejudices against
Mexicans, he concealed his feelings well. Genial and soft-spoken, Austin had

many friends among the farmers and Tejanos, but he found hard-drinking men like Jim Bowie and Sam Houston objectionable, preferring more genteel company.

When William Barret Travis and other firebrands challenged central authority in Anahuac in 1831, Austin opposed their movement until he saw the Turtle Bayou Resolutions, which proved that the colonists were merely resisting oppression. Austin became the leader of the American support for General Santa Anna, who declared adherence to the Constitution of 1824.

The leading force in the movement for a separate state for Texas, Austin carried the 1833 petition for statehood to Mexico City, hoping that President Santa Anna would intercede to grant it. Instead, Santa Anna assigned his case to the vice president, Goméz Farias. Austin quarreled with the vice president and then wrote an inflammatory letter, which caused his arrest and imprisonment. He remained a prisoner for nearly two years.

Imprisonment and injustice caused Austin to become an anti-Mexican revolutionary, and he came home to Texas in 1835 to declare that Santa Anna had betrayed the Constitution. If Texas people wanted freedom, they would have to fight for it. He was instrumental in securing the Declaration of War against Mexico, and he was chosen unanimously as the first commander of the Texas Army, a post for which he was ill-suited by temperament and experience. Within a few weeks, he left the army to become chief commissioner to the United States. After the revolution, he was appointed Secretary of State in the cabinet of President Houston, but his health had been ruined by his years in prison and he died of pneumonia a few months later.

THIS PORTRAIT OF A YOUNG STEPHEN FULLER AUSTIN IS ATTRIBUTED TO GEORGE CATLIN. *DAUGHTERS OF THE REPUBLIC OF TEXAS LIBRARY*

mining man, had the idea of settling Americans in Mexico. Austin traveled to San Antonio to see the governor. His request was at first refused, but ultimately granted by Gen. Joaquín de Arrendondo, commander for Spain in Mexico. Moses Austin secured permission to settle 300 North American families on a tract of 200,000 acres, but before he could undertake the enterprise, he died. His heir, Stephen F. Austin, managed to get the grant turned over to himself, and proceeded to become an *empresario* (a contractor hired to settle a colony). Each head of a family could buy 640 acres, plus 320 acres for each family member and 80 acres for each slave. The price was low: 12.5 cents per acre. The catch was that the settlers had to defend themselves—Austin had to raise his own militia. The government would not supply troops to protect the new colonists.

Stephen Austin chose rich bottomlands on the Colorado and Brazos Rivers. He advertised in the New Orleans newspapers for colonists, and in 1821 he chartered a ship—the *Lively*—and brought the first load of colonists to the mouth of the Brazos River. They settled at Washington-on-the-Brazos and Columbus on the Colorado.

The colonization was interrupted by the Mexican rebellion against Spain, but resumed again during the brief rule of Emperor Agostín I of Mexico (Gen. Agostín Iturbide).

By 1824, the Mexican Republic was in power under a fairly liberal constitution. The population of the Austin colonies grew to 4,000.

Under the government established in 1824, the Coahuila and Texas districts became the state of Coahuila y Texas. It was an unhappy combination: Coahuila was a mining area and Texas was agricultural. Coahuila people outnumbered Texas people five to one. And nothing that did not benefit Coahuila was passed into law.

Because of the discontent over this state of affairs, a number of immigrants from the United States decided to take the law into their own hands. They rebelled, and declared the Republic of Fredonia. This misbegotten effort was quickly suppressed by Federal troops. Stephen Austin, a member of the Coahuila y Texas legislature, led a volunteer force of new Texans loyal to Mexico who marched against Fredonia, thus demonstrating his loyalty to Mexico City.

The Fredonia rebellion had another consequence: the leaders of Mexico began to distrust the Americans who had come to Texas and decided to limit Yankee immigration. They passed a law in 1830 that effectively prevented Americans from settling in Texas, although they could put down stakes in other areas in Mexico which did not adjoin the United States. They also raised taxes, making it prohibitive to trade. When smuggling increased dramatically, the

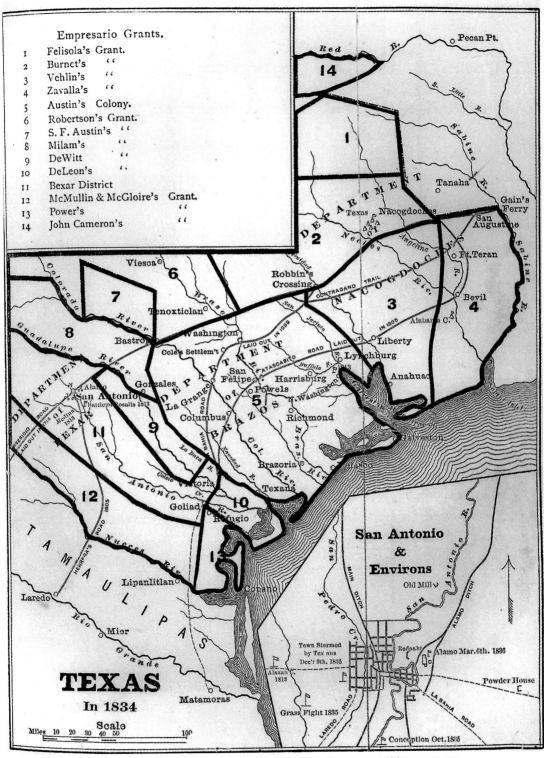

Empresario Grants.

1 Felisola's Grant.
2 Burnet's   "
3 Vehlin's   "
4 Zavalla's   "
5 Austin's Colony.
6 Robertson's Grant.
7 S. F. Austin's "
8 Milam's   "
9 DeWitt   "
10 DeLeon's   "
11 Bexar District
12 McMullin & McGloire's Grant
13 Power's   "
14 John Cameron's "

TEXAS

In 1834

Scale
Miles 10 20 30 40 50   100

THIS MAP OF *EMPRESARIO* GRANTS IN TEXAS, FROM *A PICTORIAL HISTORY OF TEXAS* BY HOMER S. THRALL, WAS PUBLISHED IN 1879.
TEXAS STATE LIBRARY & ARCHIVES COMMISSION

Federal government established customs houses to collect taxes, and big garrisons of troops to enforce the tax laws.

The Texians, as the North Americans had begun to call themselves, talked of creating a separate state of Texas in the Mexican republic. But to get statehood they would have to have a population of 80,000, and they could muster less than half that number. Meanwhile the kettle of discontent began to boil.

One story says that the lid blew off one autumn day in 1831 in Anahuac, the port on Galveston Bay. The commander of Anahuac was Col. Juan Bradburn (John Bradburn in his native Kentucky), who had joined the Mexican Army and was detested by the Texians because of his arrogance and high-handed enforcement of the tax laws. Bradburn's Mexican soldiers took their cues from him and showed their contempt for the American settlers.

Shortly before Bradburn came to town, the Texians had petitioned the governor of Coahuila y Texas to issue land titles to the people who had settled east of the San Jacinto River. The governor appointed an administrator, who chose a council and began to issue land titles.

Later, Bradburn declared the action a violation of the law of 1830 and he arrested the administrator and dissolved the council. When the citizens announced they would elect a new council, Colonel Bradburn threatened to use force to prevent it. He began to confiscate lands in the guise of enforcing the immigration restrictions, but the best of the confiscated lands became the colonel's possessions. He also commandeered the slaves of colonists to work on public buildings.

One sunny autumn day, the despotic colonel locked horns with the most aggressive man in town, William Barret Travis, a lawyer who had come from Alabama in 1831 after catching Texas fever and deserting his wife and child. In Anahuac he had joined forces with another lawyer named Patrick Jack.

One afternoon, four soldiers of the Anahuac garrison were prowling around town, looking for trouble. This was not unusual. These soldiers were *presidarios*—convict soldiers—who, according to the Texians, had been sent to Texas to show how little the Mexican government liked the Texians. The four soldiers knocked on the door of one settler and discovered a woman alone. They decided to rape her and broke into the house. The woman's screams attracted Travis, who was walking on the street with some friends. They hurried to help but the soldiers had locked the door, so they broke it down. In the excitement three of the soldiers escaped. But the principal rapist was caught and tied up. Someone suggested that they lynch the culprit. Another wanted to cut his head off and hang it on a pole at the fort.

But wiser heads prevailed. They decided to tar and feather him and take him back to the fort as an example. So someone got a bucket of tar, and the lady of the house tore up her best featherbed. The soldier was given a new coat and carried on a rail through the town to the fort.

When Colonel Bradburn learned what Travis and the others had done, he vowed that they would all be arrested for dishonoring the Mexican flag by harming a soldier. He said he would send them to Vera Cruz in chains to be tried by a military court, and he ordered a search for the men. Travis and his friends were not hard to find, and they were arrested. But arresting them and getting them to Vera Cruz were different matters. Public protest meetings were called in Anahuac and nearby communities. It was proposed that the Texians raid the fort to free the prisoners.

The colonel freed the prisoners, but the difficulties continued during the fall and winter and into the spring of 1832.

But there is another true tale which paints an entirely different picture.

"Buck" Travis took a dislike to Colonel Bradburn and tried to make his life miserable. Bradburn kept a pet bear cub; Travis brought an alligator for "bear-baiting" and the alligator chased the cub up a tree.

More serious was an incident involving two fugitive slaves from Louisiana. When their owner came to collect them, with all the paperwork done, Bradburn informed him that they were now citizens of Mexico and were serving in the Mexican Army. The slave owner engaged lawyer Travis to secure his property. When Travis failed, the lawyer developed a hatred for Bradburn.

One rainy night in May 1832, a tall man wrapped in a cloak brought a letter to the fort and then left abruptly. The letter said that a Louisiana magistrate had formed a military company of a hunded men who were going to come to Anahuac and retrieve the slaves.

For a week, the Anahuac garrison was kept on the alert as scouts searched for the invasion party. Finally Colonel Bradburn realized he had been duped and, in questioning the sentinel of the rainy night, recognized that the stranger had been Travis. A few days later Travis and his law partner were arrested. Public opinion caused the colonel to set them free but the difficulties continued.

Bradburn closed the port of Anahuac and placed the area under martial law. These draconian measures were followed by the arrest once again of many prominent citizens, including William Barret Travis and his law partner. It so happened that all those arrested were members of the War Party, which was dedicated to securing independence for Texas.

They demanded to know the charges against them, but Colonel Bradburn refused to reveal them. The protesters laid plans for a raid on the fort, but Bradburn had agents throughout the town and soon knew their plans. He moved the prisoners to an old brick kiln which he had fortified and manned with his convict soldiers. The prisoners were shackled to the ground with leg irons, and the soldiers had two field pieces at their disposal.

Another protest rally was assembled and the speakers threatened to raid the brick kiln. In response, Bradburn said he would execute the prisoners.

John Austin, a leader of the group, organized a party to go to Brazoria for help. The rescue committee set out for Brazoria, sixty miles away. Their objective was a schooner, the *Brazoria*, owned by William Russell, a trader turned smuggler. The *Brazoria* mounted two guns and a blunderbuss, a large handheld weapon that fired a heavy charge.

They next boarded the schooner and Captain Russell sailed down the river and north to Galveston Bay to attack the garrison at Anahuac, which was guarded by Fort Velasco. John Austin went ashore and asked Lt. Col. Domingo de Ugartechea, the fort commander, to let them pass. When Ugartechea refused, Austin called a council of war where the relief force was camped. That force had grown to more than a hundred men since it left Anahuac—two forty-seven-man companies and one eighteen-man company. The leaders made a plan to attack the fort and then marched down the east side of the Brazos to a point a few miles from the fort, where they camped. The men went out to collect guns and ammunition while their leaders, joined by an Irish priest, went to argue again with Ugartechea.

The colonel still refused to let them pass.

Austin told the priest to wait until the next day. Then he would see.

On June 24, 1833, the schooner sailed back up the river and took aboard the eighteen-man company of riflemen. On the evening of June 25, Captain Russell was to sail back down the river and take position opposite the fort, which stood 150 yards from the river and an equal distance from the gulf shore. The defense consisted of parallel rows of posts driven into the sand and filled with earth and rocks and shells. That was the outer wall. Inside was an embankment on which riflemen could stand and shoot without exposing anything but their heads. In the center stood a higher elevation occupied by the fort's artillery and protected by bulwarks. Between the fort and the sea was a lodgement of driftwood thrown up by the tides.

Night fell, and Captain Russell began his voyage downstream. Henry Brown, the leader of one company, began his move forward. He was to head first east and then southwest, then take cover behind the driftwood while John Austin's company approached from the north. Each of his men had a portable palisade, consisting of a three-inch plank supported by a leg. When Brown and his men got into position they were to draw the fort's fire while the Austin company set up. But just before midnight one of Brown's men tripped and accidentally fired his weapon, and the battle began. The guns of the fort flashed in the night and Brown's men could see them without exposing themselves. But Austin's company soon realized that they had a problem: They were silhouetted against the fading light, and the fort's riflemen were peppering their positions. The portable palisades were only marginally useful; after an hour one rifleman counted 130 bullet holes in his palisade.

Some of Austin's men dug trenches. Others moved up to the shelter of the fort's walls, but found they could not see anything.

The schooner got into position and opened fire, shooting scrap metal loaded as canister (packaged rifle balls fired from cannon). The schooner fired away at the fort, and soon had the fort riflemen hiding below the ramparts and holding their weapons over their heads to fire.

On the schooner there were casualties. A man making cartridges in the cabin was literally blown apart by a cannonball from the fort that smashed in through the bulkhead.

The battle lasted for nearly nine hours. By nine o'clock in the morning two-thirds of the fort's personnel were down, killed or wounded. Particularly effective was the sharpshooting of the frontiersmen, who boasted that they could shoot the eye out of a squirrel. At the end there were not enough men left standing in the fort to man the guns. Seeing this, Colonel Ugartechea surrendered.

The result of this first encounter between the military forces of Mexico and the *norteamericano* colonists was a decided colonist victory: The colonists had seven men killed and twenty-seven wounded; the Mexicans had forty-two killed and seventy wounded.

But the issue was not yet settled. The colonists had defied authority; whether it was duly constituted authority or abuse of authority remained to be decided.

The colonists held a mass meeting at Turtle Bayou, between Brazoria and Anahuac on the Brazos River, and drew up a series of resolutions. They wanted to make it clear that they had rebelled against abuse of authority. They were encouraged in this because Colonel Bradburn and the other officials of Texas were appointees of President Anastasio Bustamante, who was struggling with

Gen. Antonio de López de Santa Anna, a painting based on a daguerreo-type from about 1850.
UT Institute of Texan Cultures at San Antonio

General Santa Anna for control of Mexico. The colonists favored Santa Anna because he seemed to stand behind the Constitution of 1824, which Bustamante was against.

After the meeting, the colonists prepared to attack Anahuac and put an end to Colonel Bradburn's abuses, but higher authority intervened in the person of Col. José de las Piedras, commander of the district. He was also Bradburn's superior. The colonists made their case to Colonel de las Piedras, and he agreed that Bradburn had exceeded his authority. He promised to free the arrested men and to arrest Colonel Bradburn. Martial law was rescinded, and the colonists were reimbursed for the property Bradburn had wrongfully confiscated. After Travis and Jack were released, the colonists dispersed, and Bradburn resigned and fled to the United States. He barely escaped with his life.

Empresario Stephen Austin, the most important figure among the colonists, was in Mexico City on business when he learned of the Anahuac Incident; at first he was distressed by the actions of his compatriots, but when he learned of the Turtle Bayou Resolutions and the outcome—the punishment and flight of Colonel Bradburn—Austin was satisfied. A peace-loving man, he wanted his fellow colonists to be good citizens of Mexico. He felt they were on the right track. Like the others, Austin believed in Santa Anna.

The colonists had won a victory, but they had defied Colonel Bradburn, the appointee of the Bustamante government, and it remained to be seen what view Bustamante would take of Colonel de las Piedras's actions. Fortunately they were 1,500 miles from Mexico City, and Mexico was just then involved in civil war. Gomez Pedrazza, the elected president, had been deposed by Vicente Guerrero, who had in turn been deposed by Bustamante. Colonel de las Piedras was a Bustamante appointee. To a man, the American colonists supported Santa Anna and had since the Spanish invasion of 1829. Gen. Antonio López de Santa Anna had met the Spaniards at Tampico and driven them from the Mexican shore, becoming a national hero. No one honored him more than did these *norteamericanos.*

After the confrontations at Anahuac and Fort Velasco, the colonists pledged themselves to Santa Anna. They also decided that Colonel de las Piedras must do the same or leave Texas. At Anahuac they had organized into military companies, and now they sent a delegation to call on the colonel at his headquarters in Nacogdoches and demand his support for Santa Anna. The answer was a polite "no."

On the night of August 1, three hundred armed men camped in a glen near the town. That night all the civilian families evacuated the place, and the next morning the men marched into Nacogdoches. There was no trouble until they reached the center of the town, where they were charged by a hundred Mexican Army cavalry led by Colonel de las Piedras. The Texians took shelter behind houses and fences and fought back, losing three men. The Mexican casualties were higher because of the excellent marksmanship of the frontiersmen. When darkness fell and the fighting was suspended, de las Piedras decided to retreat to San Antonio, and his cavalry set out along that road.

That night Col. James Bowie and his band of San Antonio aristocrats joined the fight. They were all mounted, so they elected to take a cross-country short cut and cut off the de las Piedras force while the main body pursued along the road.

Bowie's group got ahead of the de las Piedras column and attacked just west of the Angelia River. In the first wild skirmish, a Mexican sergeant named Marcos was killed. Seeing that he would be defeated and captured, de las Piedras surrendered command to his deputy, who at once declared for Santa Anna, and the fight was over. Bowie's cavalry then escorted the Mexicans to San Antonio. A few days later, de las Piedras left for Mexico. The colonists rejoiced. They believed that General Santa Anna would help them in their pursuit of independence within the Mexican Republic.

TWO

※

Santa Anna

The American colonists of Texas supported General Santa Anna because they believed he stood for the Constitution of 1824, under which the *norteamericanos* hoped to achieve statehood for Texas. But they did not understand the depth of Santa Anna's ambition. Even in 1832, four years before the siege at the Alamo, he was planning to become the dictator of Mexico.

The world began to hear of the ambitious Santa Anna in 1814, when the young soldier won a medal for his part in the suppression of a revolutionary attempt by Bernardo Gutierrez de Lara. The rebels sent several hundred men into Texas under American commander Augustus W. Magee. They occupied San Antonio until Madrid became conscious of the danger and dispatched an army of 3,000 men under Gen. Joaquín de

GEN. ANTONIO DE LÓPEZ DE SANTA ANNA.
BENSON LATIN AMERICAN COLLECTION,
UNIVERSITY OF TEXAS AT AUSTIN

THIS MAP OF MEXICO FROM 1827 INCLUDES THE MEXICAN POSSESSIONS OF TEXAS, NEW MEXICO, AND CALIFORNIA. NOTABLE FEATURES INCLUDE RIVERS, MOUNTAINOUS AREAS, CITIES, TOWNS, INDIAN TRIBES, AND THE SETTLEMENT OF STEPHEN F. AUSTIN.
TEXAS STATE LIBRARY & ARCHIVES COMMISSION

Arrendondo to put down the rebellion. Arrendondo's force defeated the rebels at the Battle of the Medina River, then spent several days hunting down and annihilating the survivors. That was Santa Anna's first lesson in how to treat rebellion.

Promotion did not come quickly in the Spanish forces, and Santa Anna found himself still a captain in 1820. In that year Spain was again troubled by revolutionary activity in Mexico: Vicente Guerrero was trying to throw the Spanish out of the country. Col. Agostín Iturbide was told to eliminate these rebellious forces. Iturbide, however, had ambitions of his own and double-crossed Madrid. He made a pact with Guerrero to establish a monarchy in Mexico. Iturbide would be king.

Captain Santa Anna now made something of a name for himself in dealing with the Iturbide-Guerrero rebels. He defeated one force in a pitched battle.

Antonio López de Santa Anna Perez de Lebron
1794=1876

Santa Anna was a *criollo* (Spanish nobility born in Mexico) whose family came to Mexico in the middle of the eighteenth century and settled near Vera Cruz. In 1810, when Santa Anna was twelve, he enlisted as a cadet in the regiment of Vera Cruz. Santa Anna served the Royalist cause with some valor and in 1815 was promoted to lieutenant. By 1821 he was a lieutenant colonel.

Because he showed an ability for pacification of civilians, Santa Anna was made a member of the staff of Gen. Agostín Iturbide, commander of Spain's armies in Mexico. When a liberal government came to power in Madrid, General Iturbide broke away from Spain and declared a monarchy in Mexico with himself as its emperor, Agostín 1. One of Agostín's advisors was Brigadier General Santa Anna, but after a few months Santa Anna placed himself at the head of the Republican element in the army and staged a coup. He defeated the Royalist forces and sent Agostín 1 into exile.

Santa Anna helped write the Constitution of 1824, which was one of the most liberal in the new world. Santa Anna then went into "retirement," but actually became the *éminence grise* who dominated Mexican politics for the next thirty years. In 1829, Santa Anna secured a position as a national hero by defeating Spain's effort to recover the colony of Mexico. Then came a civil war in which he vied with Anastasio Bustamante for power. Santa Anna positioned himself as defender of the Constitution of 1824, which brought the American settlers to his cause.

In 1833, as President, he began moving toward dictatorship; two years later he established himself as

GEN. ANTONIO LÓPEZ DE SANTA ANNA COMMANDED THE MEXICAN FORCES AGAINST BOTH TEXAS AND THE U.S. THIS PAINTING WAS DONE BY PAUL L'OUVRIER. *NEW-YORK HISTORICAL SOCIETY*

dictator. When the Texians rebelled, Santa Anna took personal charge of the campaign to put down the revolution. However, he made the grievous error of overkill by terrorizing and enraging the American colonists. Santa Anna murdered not only the Alamo defenders who tried to surrender but also more than 300 prisoners captured at Goliad; then he lost the War of Texas Independence at the Battle of San Jacinto, where the Mexicans were given no quarter, just as Santa Anna had decreed for the Alamo and Goliad. *El Presidente* was captured and he traded Texas independence for his life.

Santa Anna was a handsome, aristocratic figure, a womanizer whose faithful wife remained at home near Vera Cruz and ran the Santa Anna estates. When he came to San Antonio, it was rumored that the general developed a passion for a local *señorita* and paid court, only to find that her mother insisted that marriage was the only route to her daughter's bed. A staff officer saw that his general was disconsolate and suggested a ruse—the staging of a mock marriage. The ploy worked perfectly, allowing the general to spend most of the siege of the Alamo enjoying a "honeymoon." When duty finally called, Santa Anna dispatched the lady to a presidential estate. Another, more likely tale has it that Santa Anna struck up a liaison with a mulatto lady of easy virtue called The Yellow Rose of Texas; the president bestowed a purse of 2,000 pesos on her.

Between 1838 and 1846 Santa Anna was in and out of power, but the beginning of the Mexican-American War found him in exile in Cuba, dealing privately with the Americans and advising them to attack Tampico and Vera Cruz. Santa Anna offered to make a peace settlement favorable to the United States if the Americans would help restore his power. They did, but Santa Anna doublecrossed them and tried to mobilize the resources of Mexico against the U.S. Ultimately, he lost the war, which cost Mexico its claim to Texas and all the southwestern states which then became part of the U.S.

Santa Anna never learned humility. In and out of power until 1855, this mercurial figure went into exile dreaming schemes that would restore his rule. With the coming of the American Civil War, France staged a Mexican adventure, complete with an Imperial Pretender, which Santa Anna tried to join, but he was ignored. He settled in the Bahamas in 1870 and wrote memoirs long on sex and derring-do, but very short on facts. In addition to being arrogant, he was disloyal and unprincipled, and often trusted the wrong people because they flattered his ego.

Immediately thereafter he offered his services to Iturbide in exchange for a major's commission in the rebel army. Iturbide took the gambit, but the royalists countered with a promotion to lieutenant colonel. Santa Anna then demanded that Iturbide better the offer, and he won; he was promoted to full colonel in the rebel army. Thus he advanced three grades in a few weeks' time. It was the first of Santa Anna's strategic and political maneuvers.

This revolution was backed by Mexico's *criollos*—Spanish nobility born in Mexico. Iturbide wanted to be king, but the *criollos* wanted a royal figure from one of the European families. Iturbide decided to grab the crown first. He plotted with his loyal subjects, one of whom was Santa Anna, and then established the reign of Agostín 1, Emperor of Mexico. But the reign was a short one, and when Agostín 1 was sent fleeing to Europe in 1823 by Republican forces, all that remained of his rule was the flag: green to symbolize independence, white for the church, and red for the mingling of Spanish and Indian races.

One of the key figures in the successful rebellion against Agostín 1 was Brigadier General Santa Anna, who had switched sides again. He supported the Plan of Vera Cruz, which established the Republic under the Constitution enacted in 1824.

The struggle for power within the Mexican Republic came down to a fight between Anastasio Bustamante and Santa Anna. In 1832 Santa Anna triumphed. He was not ready to assume control and responsibility, however, so he installed a stooge in the presidency: Valentin Goméz Farias. For the next two years, he would pull the strings from backstage.

Because of the events at Anahuac, Santa Anna worried that the Texians were planning rebellion. He sent Gen. José Antonio Mexia with a battalion of 500 men to investigate Texian loyalty.

Canny Stephen Austin inferred the reason for their coming and set out to woo them with smiles and favors. He "just happened" to join the Mexia party at Saltillo and rode into Texas with them. In every town they were met with smiles and pledges of loyalty to Santa Anna. At his hometown of San Felipe, Austin arranged a *fandango* (banquet and dance) in honor of the general. Austin read the Turtle Bayou Resolutions. There were many toasts, and the party was a grand success.

After San Felipe, Mexia was convinced of the loyalty of the colonists to Santa Anna. He returned to Mexico City and assured Santa Anna of the Texians' allegiance.

In that summer of 1833, the representatives from all the colonies met at San Felipe. They drew up petitions to the government for revocation of the

A LAWYER WHO RELOCATED TO SAN FELIPE, WILLIAM BARRET TRAVIS JOINED
THE WAR PARTY IN OPPOSITION TO SANTA ANNA. PAINTING BY HENRY A.
MCARDLE.
TEXAS STATE LIBRARY & ARCHIVES COMMISSION

Immigration Law of 1830 and establishment of statehood. The petitions were denied by the governor in San Antonio, but the colonists were not dismayed. Santa Anna was elected president that fall; he was their friend, was he not? He stood for the Constitution of 1824, did he not?

Stephen Austin and his supporters believed that Santa Anna was with them, but the War Party did not. This group had come to distrust Mexican authority and wanted independence. One of its leaders was William Barret Travis, who had moved to San Felipe and set up law practice; others were Patrick Jack and Robert "Three-Legged Willie" Williamson. They were a voluble faction, but the Peace Party prevailed at the convention in San Felipe.

One delegate to the convention was Sam Houston of Nacogdoches. Although he had just arrived in Texas, the people of Nacogdoches chose him because of his reputation. Houston was by far the most distinguished man at the convention. He had been elected to Congress from Tennessee and later elected governor of Tennessee. As for military experience, he had served under Andrew Jackson as an officer in the U.S. Army during the brief but bloody Creek War. He was not much of a figure in his greasy buckskins and Indian blanket, and he got drunk a lot, honoring the name "Big Souse" that the Cherokees had conferred on him when he lived with them in years past. But he displayed a sense of humor and an air of authority.

Sam Houston was not everyone's cup of tea. One of Stephen Austin's close associates said of Houston that "he jarred the moral and high class emigrants who had been brought in by Austin and other *Empresarios.*" But Houston's leadership qualities were undeniable, and he was appointed chairman of a committee to draw up a constitution for the state of Texas.

As leader of the Peace Party, Stephen Austin was chosen to take the petition for statehood to Mexico City. When Austin arrived in the capital in the summer of 1833, Mexico City was alive with intrigue and political confusion:

JUDGE ROBERT MCALPIN WILLIAMSON, KNOWN AS "THREE-LEGGED WILLIE," WAS AN INFLUENTIAL TEXAS LEADER AND A MEMBER OF THE WAR PARTY. *UT INSTITUTE OF TEXAN CULTURES AT SAN ANTONIO*

Santa Anna was still playing musical chairs with his government, remaining in the background while he issued orders. Currently he was using Vice President Goméz Farias as cat's-paw. Austin wanted to see Santa Anna but he was sent to see Vice President Farias. The interview was not successful; Austin presented his petition, and Farias told him it would be rejected out of hand. He was told to wait until Texas's population increased.

Both men lost their tempers. Austin left, still angry, and went back to his rooms and wrote a letter to the council in San Antonio urging his Tejano friends—as native-born Mexicans—to take the lead in separating Texas from Coahuila.

Austin then met with Santa Anna several times, and the meetings were most cordial. Santa Anna again mentioned the population requirement as the sticking point of Texas statehood. He did, however, agree to repeal the Immigration Law of 1830, reduce taxes, and grant the right of trial by jury. So when Austin started home he felt he had not fared badly. But before he had crossed the Rio Grande, he was arrested without warning at Saltillo. He was thrown into jail and taken back to Mexico City. There, he was hurled into a cell in an old prison from the Inquisition era. He spent six months in solitary confinement in that cell, which was sixteen feet long and thirteen feet wide with a skylight but no window. He had no idea as to the reason for his arrest, and he could talk to no one but his jailers. Later Austin learned that his letter to the council of San Antonio had been intercepted by the postmaster, who had turned it over to General Vicente Filisola, commander of the Eastern district of Mexico, as possibly treasonous. Filisola had thought so too, which was why Austin was arrested.

Austin sat in his lonely cell until April 1834, when Santa Anna suddenly ordered him sent to a city jail. There he remained for another eight months until he was released from jail on Christmas Day, 1834, and paroled to remain in the Mexico City area. He was not released to return to Texas until July 1835, two years after his arrival in the capital. He was not pardoned, but he was released in a general amnesty for criminals. By that time, both Santa Anna and the Texians had plans for Texas.

THREE

The Revolutionary Spirit Rises

In the two years that Stephen Austin had spent in Mexico City jails, the attitudes of Mexican authorities and Texians had both hardened.

In April 1834, President Santa Anna decided that the time had come to take absolute power. He made a triumphal march on Mexico City and removed Vice President Farias from office, then invoked the emergency provisions of the Constitution of 1824, dissolved Congress and began to rule by decree. The state of Zacatecas rebelled and called out its militia. Santa Anna marched north, and in the spring of 1835 he attacked Zacatecas. He won a bloody battle, and in retaliation against the citizenry for being so bold as to rebel, turned the town over to his soldiers to rape and loot for three days.

Santa Anna was determined to establish central control of his government, to do away with Federalism. One of his first steps was to send his brother-in-law, Gen. Martín Perfecto de Cós, to Saltillo, capital of the state of Coahuila y Texas, to put an end to the corruption which had rotted the pillars of that state. The governor and the legislature were deeply involved in land speculation and

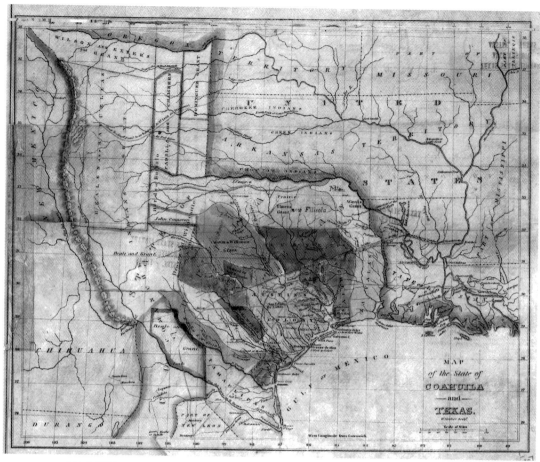

AN 1836 MAP OF THE STATE OF COAHUILA Y TEXAS SHOWS TERRITORIES IN
BOTH MEXICO AND THE UNITED STATES. UNUSUAL DETAILS INCLUDE INDIAN
TRIBES AND VILLAGES AND HERDS OF WILD HORSES, CATTLE, AND BUFFALO.
TEXAS STATE LIBRARY & ARCHIVES COMMISSION

had handed out thousands of acres of state lands. These were sold to *norteamer-icanos* at such scandalous prices that even the American colonists were shocked.

In June 1835, General Cós arrested the governor and invoked martial law in Saltillo. He arrested several legislators and land speculators, including Ben Milam, a filibuster from Kentucky who had settled near Austin's land. One speculator who was not caught was Jim Bowie, who spread the rumor that the general was planning to put the whole state under martial law. New customs regulations were ordered for Anahuac, and a new military commander was brought in, Capt. Don Antonio de Tenorio. New regulations, stronger enforcement of the tax laws—all this was threatened by the government. But the citizens of the area continued their smuggling.

On the Fourth of July, "Three-Legged Willie" Williamson of the Texian

Martín Perfecto de Cós
1800–1854

Martín Perfecto de Cós was General Santa Anna's brother-in-law, which is why he rose in the Mexican military service to high rank. Cós had the abilities of a battalion commander, but he was not suited to lead an army. He was a *criollo* who joined the army as a youth and showed promise in his first few years. After he married Santa Anna's sister, however, he rose rapidly.

A lean, handsome man with long sideburns and a dashing mustache, Cós had political clout in his native Tehuantepec. He became one of Santa Anna's principal advisors, which is probably why Santa Anna lost the War of Texas Independence. Cós was a political general with very limited military vision and no sense of strategy. He performed admirably in the cleanup of the land fraud scandals of Coahuila y Texas in 1835, but his army of 1,500 lost San Antonio that same year to a Texian force of less than 300 men.

After his defeat at San Antonio, Cós promised to cross the Rio Grande and not bring his army back to Texas, but the promise was not kept. General Santa Anna scolded his brother-in-law for losing the battle, but more for his promise to the rebels, which he ordered him to disregard. Cós brought his army back to Texas as part of Santa Anna's Army of Operations, but his units played no major role in the battles. Later, he failed to distinguish himself in the Mexican-American War.

IN JULY 1835, GEN. MARTÍN PERFECTO DE CÓS WAS SENT TO COAHUILA Y TEXAS TO STAMP OUT CORRUPTION IN THE LAND OFFICE. THE GOVERNOR AND SEVERAL LEGISLATORS WERE ARRESTED FOR THE ILLEGAL SALE OF PUBLIC LANDS. *BENSON LATIN AMERICAN COLLECTION, UNIVERSITY OF TEXAS AT AUSTIN*

THE BRIGADIER GENERAL

MARTIN PERFECTO DE COS,

Commanding General and Inspector of the Eastern Internal States.

IN THE NAME OF THE PRESIDENT OF THE REPUBLIC:

I MAKE it known to all and every one of the inhabitants of the three departments of Texas, that whenever, under any pretext whatsoever, or through a badly conceived zeal in favor of the individuals who have acted as authorities in the state, and have been deposed by the resolution of the Sovereign General Congress, any should attempt to disturb the public order and peace, that the inevitable consequences of the war will bear upon them and their property, inasmuch as they do not wish to improve the advantages afforded them by their situation, which places them beyond the uncertainties that have agitated the people of the centre of the Republic.

If the Mexican Government has cheerfully lavished upon the new settlers all its worthiness of regard, it will likewise know how to repress with strong arm all those who, forgetting their duties to the nation which has adopted them as her children, are pushing forward with a desire to live at their own option without any subjection to the laws. Wishing, therefore, to avoid the confusion which would result from the excitement of some bad citizens, I make the present declaracion, with the resolution of sustaining it.

Matamoros, July 5, 1835.

Martín Perfecto de Cós.

War Party made a fiery speech in San Felipe calling for war. "Let us no longer sleep in our posts," he said. "Let us prepare for War ... Liberty Or Death."

The speech was greeted with indifference by San Felipe's citizens but with attention by General Cós, who sent a messenger to Captain Tenorio. Actually the messenger had two messages. The first was a public proclamation which was read to the people:

"Order has been restored and all is well," it said.

But the second message, for Tenorio's private eyes, was quite different: "Be patient. Heavy reinforcements from Zacatecas are on the way. In a very short time the affairs of Texas will be settled."

Somehow the courier's saddlebags got into the hands of the Texians, and they read both messages. Most Texians at this point were busy with their crops and not concerned with revolution, but when they heard about this official duplicity they were angry. A group met and passed a resolution that authorized William Barret Travis to capture Anahuac.

Travis decided to act. He rounded up a bunch of his well-liquored friends and set out for Anahuac. When they got there, they descended on the garrison and demanded that the soldiers surrender and get out of Texas. Captain Tenorio asked for time to decide.

"You have fifteen minutes," Travis said. "If you do not surrender in that time every man will be put to the sword."

Captain Tenorio surrendered his force. The Texians seized sixty-four muskets, ammunition, and supplies, and escorted the Mexican soldiers to the road that led to the Rio Grande. Then they returned to San Felipe. But the people of San Felipe greeted Travis and his men with scorn. He had gone too far; the general populace did not want war. Seven different communities passed resolutions saying they did not want their rights defended in such a manner. Travis published in the local paper a sort of apology, in which he asked his compatriots not to be too quick to judge his activities. In a meeting in San Felipe, several peace commissioners were elected and sent to make their peace with General Cós. But Cós was not in a conciliatory mood.

General Cós sensed the public disapproval of Travis's action and decided to make an example of him and several of his friends, including Three-Legged Willie and Lorenzo de Zavala, a Tejano supporter of the Texians. They were arrested, and it was reported in the community that they would be court-martialed and shot.

The pendulum of public opinion swung the other way, and the War Party gained many adherents. Texians began to fear that Cós was about to impose martial law. The Zacatecas Massacre was fresh in their minds. Communities began to organize Committees of Public Safety. On August 20, the Columbia committee proposed a consultation meeting of all committees in San Felipe in October. The emotions of Texians were running high; all that was needed to set the flames burning was a spark. Then, on September 1, 1835, an angry Stephen Austin came home to Texas.

It was a changed Austin who stepped off the ship onto the dock at Brazoria. This mild, mid-sized bachelor had grown thinner. A year and a half in Santa Anna's custody had toughened him, however, and converted him from a peace-loving citizen who admired President Santa Anna into a firebrand who hated the Mexicans and wanted war.

A week after his arrival, friends gave a great public banquet for him in Brazoria. A thousand people jammed the ballroom to hear him speak.

"The fact is," he declared, "we must and we ought to become part of the United States. Each man with his rifle or musket would be of great use to us—very great indeed."

He called for a general consultation. Santa Anna was destroying the people's rights, he said, and they must be prepared to resist. "There will be no liberalism. If you want independence you will have to fight for it," he said.

Strange words, coming from the mouth of this mildest of men.

Home at last in San Felipe, Austin took the chair of the San Felipe Municipal Committee of Public Safety. A few days later, a courier brought word from San Antonio that General Cós had landed at the port of Copano on the Brazos with 400 troops and had begun a march to San Antonio to reinforce Colonel Ugartechea's garrison. Austin put out a call to arms.

"War is our only resource," he said. "There is no other remedy but to defend our rights, our country, and ourselves by force of arms."

This message was sent out to the Texas *ayuntamientos* (town councils) on September 19, 1835. Austin assumed the rank of general and the command of the Texas Army.

In San Antonio, as Colonel Ugartechea waited for General Cós, he prepared to carry out the new policy of the federal government—disarm the Texians.

FOUR

❧

The Battle of Gonzales

All the excitement began over a demand for the return of a cannon.

It was an old six-pound, brass-bound gun which in 1831 had been lent by the Mexican army garrison at San Antonio to the citizens of Gonzales for protection against Indian raids. As a weapon it was not much; it had been spiked after its capture from the Republican Army of 1813. That meant the powder hole in the back of the cannon had been blocked and the only way the gun could be fired was by laying a wick along the muzzle. It was used almost entirely for display to impress the Indians but was occasionally fired from the log fort overlooking the ferry crossing when Indians came along. Its firing warned the people of Gonzales that the Indians were about.

Now, four years later in 1835, Colonel Ugartechea, who had come up from Fort Velasco to command the San Antonio garrison, was asking for the cannon's return. He needed it, he said, to defend San Antonio against Mexico's enemies.

The Gonzales colonists laughed. The colonel had dozens of guns better than this one. They knew the real reason: The word had gotten out that General

Santa Anna intended to disarm the people of Texas. This was to be the first step; that's why the colonel demanded the return of the cannon.

Alcalde (Mayor) Andrew Ponton had taken a straw vote then and learned that all but three colonists were opposed to giving up the gun. So they buried it in a peach orchard at the west end of the town. Warned of impending danger, the people of Gonzales consolidated their resources. And on September 27, the *alcalde* sat down and wrote a letter to Colonel Ugartechea:

> Excellent Sir:
>
> I received an order, purporting to have come from you, for a certain piece of ordnance which is in this place. It so happened I was absent when it was delivered and in consequence the men who bore the dispatch were necessarily detained until today for an answer.... Nor do I know, without further information, how to act. This cannon was, as I have been informed, given in perpetuity to this town for its defense against the Indians. The dangers which existed in the time when we received the cannon still exist...

And he respectfully declined to return the cannon.

The citizens of Gonzales were worried. Week after week, they learned of President Santa Anna's assumption of dictatorial powers. The Constitution of 1824 had been sacked, and the legislature of Coahuila y Texas had been dissolved. They had learned the cost of resistance when the city of Zacatecas had been raped and many of its citizens killed for resisting Santa Anna.

Through an intermediary, Ugartechea had assured Gonzales that he had no intention of sending troops, but the colonel demanded the return of the only cannon the town possessed.

Their fears were soon realized.

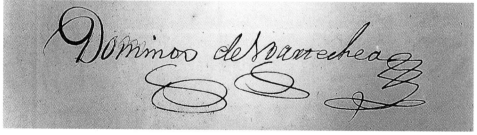

FACSIMILE SIGNATURE OF COL. DOMINGO UGARTECHEA, COMMANDER OF THE GARRISON AT SAN ANTONIO.
BENSON LATIN AMERICAN COLLECTION, UNIVERSITY OF TEXAS AT AUSTIN

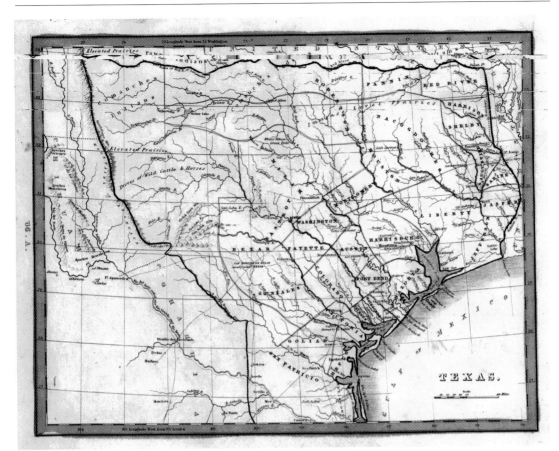

THIS MAP COVERS MOST OF TEXAS, EXCLUDING THE PANHANDLE. IN ADDITION TO
DETAIL ON RIVERS, MOUNTAINOUS AREAS, COUNTIES, CITIES, AND TOWNS, IT
SHOWS FORTS, COPPER MINES, AND INDIAN TRIBES AND VILLAGES.
TEXAS STATE LIBRARY & ARCHIVES COMMISSION

On receipt of the mayor's letter, Ugartechea sent Lt. Francisco Castañeda with a hundred cavalrymen to Gonzales to recover the cannon. On the road on September 29, they met members of the original squad sent by Ugartechea to demand the cannon. The soldiers reported that the Texians were massing at Gonzales and that they were armed.

Lieutenant Castañeda pressed on; in the afternoon his advance party reached the west bank of the Guadalupe River. The colonists were on the other side, and they had taken all the river's boats and barges, so there was no way the lieutenant's force could cross here. And the river was swollen by recent rains.

The lieutenant sent a man down to the riverbank to request a meeting with the mayor, but the messenger was told that the mayor was not there.

The Mexican column reached the riverbank the next morning. They were met by colonist Joseph Clements, who said he could speak for the *alcalde.*

Castañeda and Clements began shouting at each other across the river, an imperfect method of communication. Finally the colonists let a soldier swim the river with a message, but the return answer was that the cannon would not be given up.

Lieutenant Castañeda's force retired from the riverbank that night, while on the other shore the colonist ranks swelled. On the morning of October 1, Castañeda moved seven miles upstream to a ford. The colonists assembled on the other side and talked about attack. The cannon appeared; it had been dug up from the peach orchard and mounted on a pair of wheels borrowed from a cotton wagon. Now it was adorned with a flag, made by two young women of the town from sheeting—a six-foot length of white cloth inscribed with the legend "COME AND TAKE IT."

The air was still. The Texians thought the Mexicans were stalling, but actually, Lieutenant Castañeda's orders were to demand the gun and await developments. He was to avoid any engagement with a superior force that would cause the Mexican government any embarrassment.

After waiting a while the Texians took the initiative and forded the river. First came fifty mounted men, then the cannon with its flag, and then the rest on foot—a force now swollen to 300. Notable among the mounted men was the Reverend W. P. Smith, a Methodist preacher from Rutersville, on a white mule.

At about three o'clock in the morning, the Texians approached the Mexican position. It was a dark night and the fog lay close to the ground; somewhere a dog barked and a sentry fired, wounding one of the Texians. But it was so dark and so foggy that the soldiers of one side could not see the other, so they sat down to wait for daylight. When it came and the fog lifted the Texians found themselves in a field of corn and watermelons with the Mexican position about 300 yards away. The Texians began to move forward. The Mexican cavalry moved forward too, and the Texians fell back into the woods that lined the riverbank. Lieutenant Castañeda and Col. John Moore, the Texian commander, met in the middle of the field.

Lieutenant Castañeda said he had been ordered to retrieve the cannon and Colonel Moore invited him to come and take it, but Castañeda said he was not ordered to attack. The two looked at each other blankly and then returned to their respective sides.

The Texians loaded the gun and fired—the first shot of the Texian Revolution—a charge of scrap metal, delivered in a cloud of smoke.

The Texians then fired their rifles and made a charge against the Mexican lines, but stopped short without actually closing. Lieutenant Castañeda

A WOODCUT OF SAN ANTONIO DE BÉXAR.
TEXAS STATE LIBRARY & ARCHIVES COMMISSION

immediately retreated and headed toward San Antonio. He sustained one casualty. One Texian had received a minor gunshot wound, and another had a bloody nose caused by the rearing of a horse when the cannon was fired.

Thus ended the Battle of Gonzales. Later it would be celebrated as "The Lexington of Texas," and the smoky ejection of the cannon would be called "the Texas shot heard 'round the world."

After the confrontation at Gonzales, the Texians moved back to the town. They expected another attack soon. Colonel Ugartechea had 500 men in San Antonio with two working cannon.

The Texians knew that General Cós was on his way with reinforcements but they also expected reinforcements of their own.

One Gonzales colonist, David McComb, wrote:

> Let our citizens come on—the spirit is up among us and victory and independence certain. San Antonio once taken and garrisoned by our troops, no hostile Mexican would dare put his foot in Texas.
>
> We are well supplied with beef and bread and corn for our horses. We have a grist mill....and we are now in abundance. We shall grind plenty of meal in advance for those who are coming in.
>
> The Anglo-American spirit appears in everything we do: quick, intelligent and comprehensive. While such men are fighting for their rights, they may possibly be overpowered by numbers, but if whipped, they won't stay whipped.

FIVE

❧

Tilting Toward War

W hen the Texians had seen the last of the dust of the Castañeda force, they stopped to consider their situation. They had possession of the field and they had acquired a considerable amount of military baggage and some horses left by the Mexicans. They marched back to Gonzales, where they arrived at about two o'clock in the afternoon. They were expecting a Mexican attack at any moment. They talked about Colonel Ugartechea and the reinforcements coming to him; they expected him to appear with a large force of men and cannon and try to burn Gonzales to the ground. As for themselves, they expected another 150 reinforcements, and if they were not attacked, they would march on San Antonio.

On October 3, a skilled blacksmith arrived at Gonzales, and they told him how the cannon had smoked furiously at the breech. The smith took the cannon back to his shop and heated it. He poured molten metal into the oversized touchhole. Then he bored a second touchhole ahead of the first one. But it proved to be too small to deliver enough oxygen to fire the gun, so he plugged it

Benjamin Rush Milam
1788=1835

Ben Milam was born in Frankfort, Kentucky in 1788. He fought in the War of 1812, and was one of the earliest American settlers to go to Texas, arriving in 1818 and becoming a Mexican citizen. In 1819, he fought in the Mexican Army against the Spanish.

He later joined a filibustering expedition, and was captured by government troops and jailed. Freed in 1825, he applied for an *empresario* grant, but did not receive it. He then began settling Americans on other men's grants. In 1834, Milam went to Saltillo to secure a land commissioner to grant title to these lands when he was arrested and jailed as a land speculator in General Cós's cleanup campaign. He escaped from prison in September 1835 and rode 400 miles back to Texas.

Milam then joined the Collinsworth band in the attack on La Bahía, and later signed on with Gen. Stephen Austin's army for the siege of San Antonio. He was commissioned as a scout and left on a scouting mission outside San Antonio. When he returned on December 4, he found that the command had changed—Austin had left and Edward Burleson was in charge. Burleson was just about to lift the siege and retreat to Goliad for the winter when Milam arrived and objected.

Burleson said if Milam could find enough volunteers, he could attack San Antonio, so Milam left the tent, waved his hat, and said, "Who will go with old Ben Milam to San Antonio?" Three hundred men volunteered, and that night they assembled and prepared the attack. Before dawn on December 5, 1835, they attacked San Antonio. Milam was killed by a Mexican sniper on the third day of the assault and was buried just a few steps from where he fell in the courtyard of the Veramendi House. He was the first hero of the Texas Revolution.

A PAINTING OF BEN MILAM, WHO WAS KILLED LEADING THE TEXIANS IN THE BATTLE OF BÉXAR.
TEXAS STATE LIBRARY & ARCHIVES COMMISSION

up with metal. He used the point of a file to centerpunch the original touch-hole. About fifteen degrees from the spike he bored a new touchhole, brushed the cannon, and mounted it on wooden trucks cut from cottonwood trees they found near the river. He also attached a limber to the trail of the cannon.

"She's finished," the smith announced. "Now all you have to do is name her."

So they christened the gun the Flying Artillery and prepared to take her into action.

The news of the victory at Gonzales spread throughout the Texas settlements. Sam Houston, Frank Johnson (a prominent member of the War Party), Stephen Austin, James Bowie, William Barret Travis, and James Fannin all hurried to Gonzales. All but Austin were seeking leadership of the Texas Army. Fannin and Houston had the best credentials. Fannin had spent two years at the United States Military Academy at West Point. Houston, as noted, had served in the United States Army. He had also just been appointed commander of the troops of Nacogdoches district, because he was a former American army officer. On October 8, he issued a stirring proclamation:

> The morning of Glory is dawning upon us. The work of Liberty has begun. Let your valor proclaim to the world that Liberty is your birthright. We cannot be conquered by all the arts of anarchy and despotism combined. In heaven and in valorous hearts we repose our confidence.

Events were moving rapidly that October. A band of volunteers under Capt. George Collinsworth was racing across country from the Colorado River to attack General Cós because they thought he had a war chest containing $50,000 to pay the troops at San Antonio. En route they picked up Ben Milam, a longtime resident of Texas who had just escaped from jail after being arrested by General Cós as a land speculator. They missed Cós, but attacked and captured the Presidio of La Bahía outside Goliad.

Within a week the colonists had scored two victories. The importance of this one was that it cut General Cós off from the port of Copano. Hereafter he would have to get his supplies over the land route across the northern Mexico desert.

The question at Gonzales was: Who would lead the Texas Army? James Bowie and James Fannin both had support, and Sam Houston had none. But the colonists chose Stephen Austin, the most unlikely candidate, despite the fact

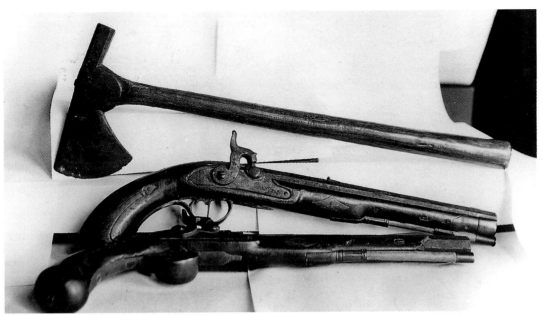

GEN. STEPHEN AUSTIN'S PERSONAL PISTOLS AND TOMAHAWK FROM THE 1835 SIEGE OF SAN ANTONIO.
CENTER FOR AMERICAN HISTORY, UNIVERSITY OF TEXAS AT AUSTIN

that he had no military experience. When he arrived at Gonzales, there was no doubt about it; he was voted in by acclamation. Sam Houston accepted a subordinate position and went off to San Felipe to the convention that had been called to consider the issues before the colonists.

Now the war fever spread to America, spurred by a combination of sympathy for Texas and adventurism. The citizens of New Orleans held a mass meeting and pledged money for arms. That same day two 100-man companies assembled in the city, and a few hours later left for Texas. They were called the New Orleans Greys and the Mobile Greys. They were adventurers, not soldiers, and the only thing military about them was their gray uniforms.

On October 12, 1835, General Austin led his troops out from Gonzales. They had expected an attack from Colonel Ugartechea, but it had not come. They were marching to assault San Antonio. The column moved out with the Come and Take It flag flying at the head and the Flying Artillery just behind, drawn by two teams of longhorn steers.

A volunteer described the scene:

> Buckskin breeches were the nearest approach to uniform, some being soft and yellow, others, from long familiarity with rain and grease and dirt, had become hard, black, and shiny. Some men wore

shoes and some wore moccasins. Here a broadbrimmed sombrero overshadowed the military cap at its side, the tall bearskin helmet rode beside a coonskin cap with the tail hanging down behind ... big American horses, nimble Spanish ponies ... half broken mustangs ... sober mules ...

The only piece of equipment common to all the men was their water bottles: In lieu of a canteen, every man carried a Spanish gourd.

When they were half a day out of Gonzalez the wooden axles and wheels of the Flying Artillery began to smoke. They poured water over the axles to cool them; the result was palliative but not permanent. They tried greasing the axle with tallow: The result was the same. As the army reached Sandies Creek, the teamsters reported that breakdown was imminent. They camped on the west side of Sandies Creek and the Flying Artillery barely made it; it broke down as they pitched camp.

Next morning, General Austin and Ben Milam inspected the artillery, decided the cannon was beyond repair, and buried it by the roadside.

The column went on. General Austin appointed Ben Milam to command a mounted company to reconnoiter campsites. When they got to Cibolo Creek they discovered the trail of a hundred mounted men. General Austin sent other units to find the enemy.

On October 19, the Tejano Juan Seguín rode into camp with information: Many Tejanos wanted to join the army, he said. General

JUAN SEGUÍN. PORTRAIT BY THOMAS JEFFERSON WRIGHT, PAINTED IN 1838. *TEXAS STATE LIBRARY & ARCHIVES COMMISSION*

Juan Seguín
1806-1890

Juan Seguín was one of the leaders of the Tejanos who joined the Texas revolution. He came from a prominent San Antonio *criollo* family which was liberal in outlook and objected to Santa Anna's centralization of power. For a time Juan was provisional *alcalde* of San Antonio; his father had been a political ally of Stephen Austin.

In 1835, Seguín led a band of horsemen in the assault on San Antonio. He fought in the Alamo and expected to die there, but was sent out with messages calling for reinforcements and was in Goliad when the fortress fell. He was a captain of cavalry in the Battle of San Jacinto. At the end of the war, he supervised the proper burial of the remains of the heroes of the Alamo.

After Texas won its independence, he was shocked to learn that his *norteamericano* friends had short memories of his service. The real blow came in 1842, when as mayor of San Antonio he helped defeat a Mexican expedition against the city. The expedition's commander lied and said that Juan was a loyal Mexican citizen. His Texian friends were eager to believe any slur against a Tejano, and soon vigilantes forced him to flee to Mexico, where he was received with suspicion and given the choice of joining the Mexican Army or going to prison. He chose the army and remained in it until the end of the Mexican-American War.

After the war Seguín received permission to return to Texas, but in 1867 a new campaign of harassment forced his return to Mexico. He died in Nuevo Laredo, just across the Rio Grande from the land whose freedom he had fought for in 1836.

A LATER PHOTO OF COL. JUAN NEPOMUCENA SEGUÍN, MEXICAN PATRIOT TO TEXAS DURING THE REVOLUTION. *UT INSTITUTE OF TEXAN CULTURES AT SAN ANTONIO*

Austin appointed Seguín captain of cavalry and told him to raise a company of mounted soldiers.

On October 21, one of the search units, led by Lieutenant Bull, was attacked by a Mexican cavalry patrol. The Texians retreated until the enemy was only fifty yards away and then fired a rifle volley. The Mexicans retreated and the Texians chased them into Béxar. The skirmish raised the morale of the whole column. It was the first they had seen of the enemy since Gonzales.

Meanwhile General Cós had reached San Antonio de Béxar and was busy building fortifications. His men cut down trees to create fields of fire, placed cannon on the top of the church and in the streets, and prepared to resist attack.

On October 26, General Austin appointed Colonel Moore, the hero of Gonzales, to organize a cavalry command. The next day, he appointed William Barret Travis as captain to raise a company of cavalry. That day Col. James Bowie and Capt. James Fannin went on a scouting mission to find the best place for the main army to camp near San Antonio. They chose a place on a bend in the San Antonio River near the old mission of Concepción. The next morning, they were attacked by three hundred dragoons and a hundred Mexican infantry. The battle was delayed by heavy fog, and in the fog Bowie split his command. When the fog lifted, the Mexicans began to advance behind two field guns.

The Texians were short of ammunition. "Make every shot count, boys," Colonel Bowie said, and his riflemen did their best. They had an advantage: Their rifles had a range of 200 yards and the Mexican Brown Bess muskets a range of only 70 yards. The Mexican gunners began to fall, and soon so many men were killed or wounded that the guns could not be manned.

Bowie led a charge against the guns, captured the artillery, and turned it on the Mexicans. The Mexican cavalry and infantry retreated from the field. Half an hour later, General Austin came up with the main body of the army. He wanted to pursue, but Colonel Bowie reminded him that the Texians did not have any artillery.

So General Austin had to be content with a partial victory. It was their third in a row, and they had killed sixty-seven Mexicans and captured several cannon. The Texian loss was a single man.

While the Texas Army was marching, President Santa Anna was in seclusion on his estate, Manga de Clava, near Jalapa on the road to Vera Cruz. In the few months since he'd taken full power into his own hands he had made himself so hated by Mexicans that he had resigned due to "ill health" and turned the reins of government over to the Vice President, Miguel Barragán.

On November 1, the Texas Army set up camp at the old mill just north of San Antonio's main plaza.

"What we want to do now," General Austin said, "is starve them out."

The siege of San Antonio had begun.

But laying siege is tedious work, and the volunteers who made up the Texas Army had little patience for it. When the excitement ended they began drifting away, although General Austin sent out cavalry patrols every day to cover the approaches to the town. On November 6, he sent Capt. Andrew Briscoe and a company of mounted riflemen to patrol west of the city and stop any supplies from moving into San Antonio. But in this Texas army every man was a general, and after three days Briscoe decided the work was too dull. He said he was going back to camp.

Captain Travis elected to stay on and so did twelve other volunteers. The rest of the men went back to camp, and Travis was in command.

Three days later, they crossed the trail of a large herd of horses and followed. Travis found a prize—a herd of 300 horses escorted by only a handful of soldiers.

Travis ordered a charge, and the enemy disappeared. Without firing a shot, he captured the herd. When they got them to camp, they discovered that the herd was exhausted and he sent some men to escort the horses to the farm of Juan Seguín for recuperation.

While the Texas Army was preparing to attack San Antonio, serious business was in progress in San Felipe. The consultative conference was making decisions. Would they affirm loyalty to the Constitution of 1824, or would they declare the independence of Texas?

Sam Houston was there, clothed in his official trappings as leader of the Nacogdoches militia and getting drunk with Jim Bowie, who had left the dull siege of San Antonio.

The meeting began on November 3, 1835. The delegates, from every Texas settlement, voted an "Organic Law" under which they set up a provisional government, consisting of a legislature and an executive. As a sop to the War Party the firebrand Henry Smith was elected governor.

After the convention dealt with the matters of government, they considered the war. On November 12, Sam Houston was chosen as commander in chief of the Texas Army and instructed to begin raising a professional force. He was not, however, given command of the army that was besieging San Antonio.

The delegates were well aware that they would stand or fall, ultimately, on the support of the United States. So Stephen Austin, as the person best known to Americans, was chosen as the principal member of a three-man commission to go to America and seek government support.

On November 18, Stephen Austin received the news from San Felipe. But before he left for America he wanted to capture San Antonio, and a company of the Greys from New Orleans had just arrived with two cannon. General Austin proposed an attack, but his officers refused to obey his orders so he canceled them. It was with a great sense of relief that he paraded his troops for the last time three days later and prepared to step down as commander. The problem now was to save the army, to keep the men from going home. Austin asked how many would be willing to maintain the siege. Four hundred men said they would maintain the siege if they could elect their own commander. They elected Edward Burleson as their general and Frank Johnson as the second in command.

On November 25, General Austin rode out of camp bound for San Felipe and the United States, not knowing what might be the outcome of the military adventure he had begun.

SIX

❧

San Antonio

When Sam Houston was named commander in chief of the Texas Army on November 12, 1835, he was told to establish his headquarters at Washington-on-the-Brazos, fifty miles from San Felipe. His first task was to raise a professional army, using land grants as payment.

This was no easy assignment, since the number of men with military experience was very limited. On November 13, he offered the post of inspector general to James Fannin, based on Fannin's West Point experience. In a confidential letter to Fannin, Houston revealed his strategy for fighting the war against the Mexicans. Because the Texas Army had virtually no equipment, he believed that Texas must fight a defensive war at first. Fannin's post was a responsible one, second only to Houston's own. But Fannin did not want responsibility. He wanted action, and a chance to win glory.

Dr. James Grant, a Scottish filibuster, had mining interests in Mexico and he knew the area. Grant proposed that a Texas unit travel to Matamoros to join 5,000 American filibusters heading for the heart of Mexico. Even though General Houston had rejected the plan, members of the council supported it.

Matamoros, an important Mexican city of 12,000 on the south side of the Rio Grande, was the supply center for General Cós's army. At the moment the Matamoros Expedition was on hold, awaiting the outcome of the siege of San

James Walker Fannin
1804 = 1836

The illegitimate son of a Georgia physician and planter and a young woman of good family, James Walker Fannin was raised by his maternal grandfather. Appointed to the U.S. Military Academy, he left West Point after two years, settled in Georgia, and married. After a few years he moved to Texas, where he speculated in land and traded in slaves, bringing 153 slaves from Cuba on one voyage.

In Texas Fannin was a prominent member of The War Party, and he spent the winter of 1834–35 in the U.S. carrying out a campaign for an independent Texas. He took part in the earliest actions of the War of Independence, beginning with the Battle of Gonzales. After the rebel capture of San Antonio, he became a military leader. He was offered the post of Inspector General of the Army of Texas by General Houston, but he wanted action and glory so he refused the appointment.

Instead, Fannin became the commander of 450 men intended for the Matamoros Expedition, which he was to lead. His unit was holding the fort at Goliad during the siege of the Alamo when Colonel Travis called on him repeatedly for reinforcement. However, Fannin did not respond until it was too late to come to the defenders' aid. General Houston ordered him to destroy Goliad and join the main Texas Army, which he was trying to do when he fought and lost the Battle of Coleto Creek and surrendered to General Urrea. His troops and some others, numbering more than 425, were massacred by the Mexicans on Palm Sunday, 1836, and Fannin was put to death by firing squad. The massacre produced the battle cry *Remember Goliad!* with which the Texas Army went into the Battle of San Jacinto.

Fannin was an ambitious man whose abilities did not match his aspirations. He would not follow orders, and this failing led to the destruction of his command and his own death.

Antonio. In fact, Dr. Grant and Frank Johnson were deeply involved in the San Antonio siege.

The question of the moment lay with General Burleson. Was he going to carry out the attack that General Austin had wanted? Burleson wanted to continue the siege, but General Houston was pressing him to withdraw to Goliad, and his council of officers wanted to fall back to Gonzales for the winter. The imports, the American volunteers, wanted immediate action.

On the morning after Burleson took command of the army, Scout Erastus "Deaf" Smith galloped into camp to report a Mexican pack train coming into San Antonio on the old Presidio Road. The train was guarded by only a handful of soldiers.

Scout Smith suggested that the train might be carrying silver to pay the Mexican soldiers. General Burleson sent James Bowie with a party to intercept the pack train. This action came to the attention of General Cós, who in turn sent reinforcements with a field piece. In

ERASTUS "DEAF" SMITH, SAM HOUSTON'S PRINCIPAL SCOUT. HE PARTICIPATED IN VIRTUALLY EVERY ACTION OF THE TEXAS REVOLUTION. *CENTER FOR AMERICAN HISTORY, UNIVERSITY OF TEXAS AT AUSTIN*

the running skirmish called the Grass Fight that followed, the Mexicans lost about fifty men. The Texians suffered no losses and captured the pack train. When they got back to camp with the train, they discovered that the animals were carrying only grass to feed the horses. Merely a foraging party, the pack train had slipped through the Texas lines a few days earlier.

The debate about the attack on San Antonio continued. Scout Ben Milam went on a mission south of camp while the senior officers dithered. General Burleson was ready to order the retreat favored by his officers council when three Texians who had been involved in the Battle of Gonzales suddenly showed up in camp. They had been arrested by the Mexicans after the battle and taken to San Antonio and jailed as dangerous revolutionaries. They had escaped from the jail and came to join the army. They reported that the San Antonio garrison was very weak and ripe for attack. Burleson took courage in hand and gave the order to attack at dawn on December 2. The decision relieved everyone, and the camp was bustling that afternoon and evening. But in the middle of the night it was discovered that one of the scouts, Hendrick Arnold, was missing. He was Deaf Smith's son-in-law, though no one knew him very well.

Someone suggested that he might have deserted to the enemy. If so, the important element of surprise was lost. General Burleson called off the attack. The angry volunteers refused to muster for the morning parade and the muttering became louder. In the afternoon, Burleson came full circle and ordered the retreat to Goliad.

Mutiny loomed, until the missing scout appeared with a defecting Mexican Army officer in tow. The scout had sneaked into San Antonio to visit his wife and had picked up the defector in town. They reported that the Mexican camp was in even worse condition than the Texian, and that there was no suspicion that Burleson's army might attack.

At this point, Ben Milam returned from his scouting mission, furious that General Burleson had ordered a retreat. He went to Frank Johnson's tent to consult. Milam argued that they should continue the siege, and Johnson agreed. Ben Milam strode grimly out of the tent and down the road to General Burleson's tent. Burleson told him he had ordered the withdrawal on instructions from General Houston.

There was more conversation, then Milam emerged from the tent. "Who will follow old Ben Milam into San Antonio?" he asked, calling for volunteers to attack San Antonio. Three hundred men responded and he called on them to rendezvous at the old mill after dark.

The gloom of dusk had just turned to the black of night when the three hundred volunteers assembled at the old mill. A number of Tejanos under Juan Seguín were there; San Antonio was their home, and they had a personal stake in its capture.

The assault force had two field pieces: a six-pounder and a twelve-pounder. General Burleson kept about a quarter of the men in reserve under command of Colonel Neill. They would take another field piece and cross the river to make a diversionary attack on the Alamo at about three o'clock in the morning. Ben Milam kept one division of six companies and the artillery; the other division was led by Johnson. This second division consisted of eight companies, including one company of Tejanos led by Capt. Placido Benavides. Both companies were equipped with crowbars to smash their way into houses.

The attack began shortly before dawn on December 5, 1835. Ben Milam headed down Acequia Street, guided by Hendrick Arnold. Johnson, guided by Deaf Smith, headed down Soledad Street toward the Veramendi house. Neill and a gun crew took one field piece across the river into range of the Alamo. Colonel Neill's mission was the most dangerous: If the Mexicans attacked after he had crossed the river, he and his men would be in serious trouble.

An hour before dawn, Neill primed his cannon to fire the shot that would signal Milam and Johnson that it was time to attack.

Their men waited in the darkness of the town, the only sounds the whistling of the wind and the call of the sentries as they walked their rounds.

"Centinela alerta."

The tension became almost unbearable. Would the signal ever come?

At five o'clock, a cannon shot broke the stillness. The Mexican camp came suddenly to life as bugles shrilled, drums rattled, and soldiers ran to their posts. The Mexican artillery opened a barrage. Although the Texians did not know what the Mexicans were shooting at, the attack force had already taken cover.

The diversion worked perfectly. Under cover of the gunfire against the Alamo, both divisions entered the north side of the town across the river unopposed. They passed a group of sentries huddled around a fire; the Texians ignored them and went on. The one difficulty was that the firing prevented communication between divisions. Also, the carriage of the twelve-pounder was damaged in the haul through the streets, so it became useless. But they still had the six-pounder.

The Mexicans discovered the attackers as the Johnson division approached the Veramendi house. A sentry fired his musket to alert the garrison. Deaf Smith shot the sentry dead.

They got to within two hundred yards of the city plaza when the gunners began firing canister on them from concealed guns. The Mexicans had done an artful job of siting their cannon around the plaza, each in a fortified position, linked to the next by an eight-foot trench topped with a palisade of pilings and earth. The guns fired through narrow slits in the palisades. The canister hammered down the narrow streets as the Texians plastered themselves against the walls and broke into the buildings for shelter. Men, women, and children ran out of the houses into the streets in their nightclothes.

When morning came, the riflemen began to find targets. The Mexican infantrymen fired their Brown Bess muskets, but the muskets had only a seventy-yard range, and the powder charge was so light that sometimes a musketeer could score a direct hit only to have the ball bounce off its intended victim.

At close range, the Texians' double-barreled shotguns were very effective, especially when loaded with deer slugs.

Each house was a small fortress built of thick adobe and featuring few windows. The Texians fought from house to house, sometimes from room to room. When they captured a house, they secured it with sandbags and pieces of timber. But holding a house was not enough; each flat roof was surrounded by a wall two or three feet high. The Texians used ladders to get up onto the roofs and hid behind the walls for sharpshooting. But it was a two-way street: The Mexicans had their sharpshooters too, equipped with the British Baker rifle, a modern weapon with a range of 270 yards. They had manned the rooftops of many of the stronger stone houses and the belfry of San Fernando Church, which commanded a view of the city.

The siting of the artillery around the central square had been masterful. San Fernando Church in the middle of the square was a real bastion, bristling with cannon. The Texians had no cannon, and had to rely on their sharpshooting. In short order, several sharpshooters were wounded and their comrades faced the problem of getting them down off the roofs and into the houses for protection. Still, the Texian snipers were effective; several times during the day, the Mexican cannon had to be abandoned, only to be manned once more.

At the end of the day, the Texians assessed their situation. They had a foothold in the city, but no more than that.

Ben Milam and Frank Johnson counted noses. One of their contingent was dead and fifteen were wounded. Their artillery was of no use: the twelve-pounder was disabled and the six-pounder ineffective at long range. The Mexicans had all the advantage of artillery and they knew it. Their guns kept firing all night long. Many of the buildings held by the Mexicans were constructed of stone, and breaking into them without artillery was a difficult job, particularly when harried by sharpshooters from above.

That night, the Texians strengthened their positions and the Mexicans did the same. It didn't help that the defenders outnumbered the attackers three to one.

The second night of the attack on San Antonio, the two Texian divisions made contact. General Burleson visited them, bringing water and food for the hungry men. Artillery fire that night was only sporadic, which raised the morale of the attackers, but General Cós had hung the blood-red *Deguello* flag from the Alamo—no quarter asked or given.

The third morning dawned cool and crisp; once again the cannon were the focal point of the Texian riflemen. The Mexicans had the advantage of position

Edward Burleson
1798–1851

Edward Burleson was one of the many Americans who came to Texas seeking their fortune. Born in North Carolina, he moved with his family to Tennessee in 1812. Two years later, he moved to Missouri and enlisted in the militia. By 1823, he had risen to the rank of colonel. When he returned to Tennessee, Burleson joined that state's militia and soon became a colonel there as well.

During a visit to Texas in 1830, he caught "Texas fever" and moved his family there in 1831. The next year, he was elected colonel of the Texas militia. Burleson joined the Texian contingent at the Battle of Gonzales in October 1835 under the command of Gen. Stephen Austin. But when Austin ordered the attack on San Antonio on November 21, Burleson led the contingent of officers who refused to obey Austin's orders. The general was forced to revoke his orders, and the controversy convinced Austin to step down as commander of the army. Fortunately for him, the Texian Provisional Government decided at that time to send him to America as a commissioner to seek U.S. government assistance. Austin asked the troops how many would continue the siege of San Antonio; 400 said they would stay on if they could elect their own officers.

They elected Burleson as general and Frank Johnson as adjutant. The siege continued, but Burleson was indecisive and did not attack. Many of his officers wanted to break off the siege and spend the winter at Gonzales, and Burleson was ready to break camp. Then Ben Milam returned from a scouting expedition and convinced Burleson to let him call for volunteers. If enough men volunteered, Milam could lead them into San Antonio. Three hundred men answered his call, and the San Antonio attack was revived.

THIS DAGUERREOTYPE OF EDWARD BURLESON WAS TAKEN IN SAN MARCOS, TEXAS, IN 1850.
TEXAS STATE LIBRARY & ARCHIVES COMMISSION

Burleson held the headquarters camp outside San Antonio and routed a desperation attack by two columns of Mexican troops. After General Cós surrendered, General Burleson paroled the Mexican Army on the condition that they cross the Rio Grande and not return, a promise that Cós did not keep. When the San Antonio battle was over, Burleson cheerfully accepted demotion to colonel's rank and command of the 1st Texas Regiment.

He went on to fight at San Jacinto. When the battle ended in a Texian victory, Burleson and Deaf Smith carried the news of the capture of Santa Anna to General Filisola. After the war, Burleson was elected to the Texas senate and also served in the ranks of the Texas Rangers.

In 1844, Burleson ran unsuccessfully for President of the Republic. A supporter of annexation, he once again took up arms to fight in the Mexican-American War. After that war, he was elected to the Texas state senate.

and artillery, but the Texians had the advantage of better infantry weapons and superior marksmanship.

In the fighting that day, the Texians lost another man killed. Fourteen more men were wounded. A lieutenant in Ben Milam's division led a charge that captured another house. The progress was slow, but they were advancing steadily on the central plaza.

That night, Colonel Ugartechea set out for Nacogdoches with the promise to bring reinforcements back to the Mexicans. The Texas men cleaned their weapons and prepared for more hard fighting. The next morning, they were surprised to see a new redoubt on the Alamo side of the San Antonio River. Here was a threat to the Texian flank. The riflemen soon settled that problem, picking off so many Mexicans that the position was abandoned.

When Johnson's division was blocked by a fortified house, he called for a cannon. Ben Milam sent him the six-pounder. Now better armed, the men pounded away at the house until the Mexicans withdrew. With the destruction of so many houses around the plaza, the defenders were spurred into stouter resistance. In a pause in the fighting, Ben Milam summoned his officers to the Veramendi house for consultation.

He was surveying the battlefield with his glass when the reflection was spotted by a Mexican sniper in a tree by the river across from the Alamo. The rifleman took aim with his Baker rifle and fired. Ben Milam fell dead with a bullet through his head.

VERAMENDI HOUSE DOORS IN SAN ANTONIO (WHERE BEN MILAM WAS KILLED) SHOWING BULLET MARKS FROM THE BATTLE. THE HOUSE NO LONGER EXISTS. THIS PHOTO APPEARS IN *EARLY SETTLERS & INDIAN FIGHTERS OF SOUTHWEST TEXAS*.
TEXAS STATE LIBRARY & ARCHIVES COMMISSION

The Texians in the courtyard were stunned, but one of them saw the sniper in the tree and shouted. Half a dozen Texas rifles spouted, and out of the tree tumbled Felix de la Garza, "the best shot in the Mexican Army." He was dead before his body bounced off the riverbank and flopped into the river next to the Alamo.

Twenty-three-year-old Henry Karnes of Tennessee was hiding behind a building with several members of his company, avoiding the intense Mexican cannon fire. The Mexicans brought up two more field pieces and he watched them destroy the adobe wall that sheltered them. Across the road was a stone house, and occasionally they had a glimpse of a head or black shako in a window. The large number of musket barrels that protruded from the windows and roof were further evidence of Mexican occupancy.

Henry Karnes sudddenly got up and gestured toward the stone house.

"Boys," he said, "load your guns and be ready. I'm going to break down that door. I want you to pour a steady hot fire into those fellows on the roof and hold their attention until I reach the door. Then I want you to make a rush on the house."

"Don't be a damned fool," said one of his friends. "Can't you see the muzzles of all those *escopetas* (rifles) in the windows?"

"Damn the Mexicans and their *escopetas,*" Karnes shouted. "It's either that house or retreat. You men do what I tell you."

And with a crowbar in one hand and his rifle in the other, he dashed across the street to the house. The Mexican soldiers on the roof looked down on him but could not fire without exposing themselves to the rifles across the way.

Karnes pried at the door until it gave and collapsed inward. He rushed into the house, half a dozen of his men behind him. They captured a dozen prisoners whom they immediately disarmed and paroled. They hadn't enough men to guard prisoners, but there was no blood lust in their hearts, and they did not want to kill anyone unnecessarily.

The Texians' advance through the town quickened, and the hand-to-hand fighting in the streets increased in tempo. One house was occupied both by Mexicans and Texians on either side of a wall. The Texians broke a hole through the wall and were trying to fire through it when the wall collapsed onto the Mexicans. The Texians took eighteen soldiers and one lieutenant prisoner, all of whom they paroled.

On that third night, General Cós sent a squadron of cavalry in search of Colonel Ugartechea's relief column. The searchers did not find Ugartechea; in fact, they did not even look, but deserted and crossed the Rio Grande into Mexico. This was certainly an indication of the state of morale in the Mexican ranks.

The rebels were now in sight of their objective, but as they closed in, the defense grew stronger. The fourth day dawned cold and wet and both sides suffered from damp powder. The Texians were within yards of the military plaza, a position they had gained slowly, house to house. Johnson had succeeded Ben Milam as leader of the attackers; he now ordered an assault on the group of buildings known as Zambrano Row. After the assault began, the Mexicans fell back to buildings on the plaza, and General Cós moved his headquarters to the Alamo. There he formulated a daring plan. With so many Texians involved in the attack on San Antonio, their headquarters camp must be almost deserted. If Cós could capture Texian headquarters, the attack force would have to retreat to Gonzales. Cós sent a column of infantry and a squadron of cavalry to attack the Texian headquarters, but they found that General Burleson had anticipated

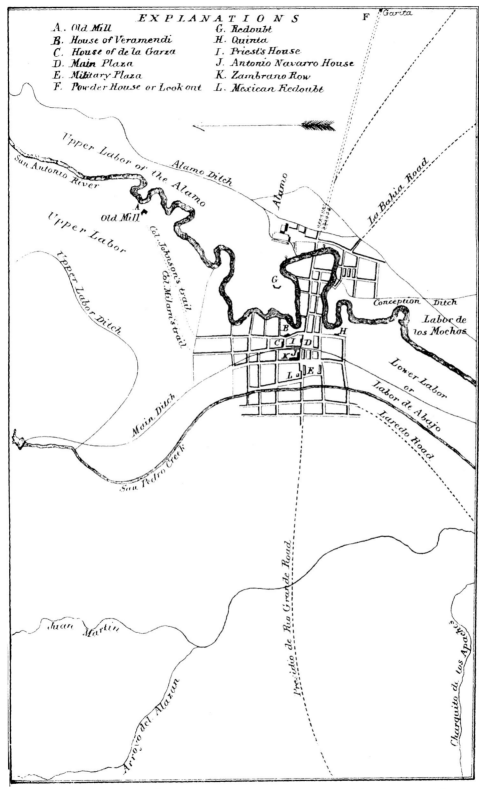

THIS MAP FROM HENDERSON YOAKUM'S 1855 *HISTORY OF TEXAS* SHOWS SAN ANTONIO AND THE SURROUNDING LAND. BEN MILAM AND FRANK JOHNSON'S PATHS DURING THE SEIGE OF THE TOWN ARE INDICATED ON THE LEFT.

them and was prepared. The Mexican infantry approached the camp from the east and the cavalry swooped down from the west, banners flying, bugles blowing, and lances flashing. Colonel Neill was waiting, his cannon packed with canister. His men opened fire and the two columns retreated back to the Alamo.

Cós's only hope now was Colonel Ugartechea, and he did not disappoint the general. On that afternoon of December 8, his relief force reached the Alamo. But it was a dismal group, mostly convict soldiers, untrained, hungry, and exhausted, and as they were unshackled they turned on the officers. They even attacked General Cós. The convict uprising was quelled, but not before several officers had been injured and Cós thoroughly roughed up.

The Battle of San Antonio continued into the evening of December 8. Colonel Johnson could see their objective, the plaza and the church. One obstacle remained: the building known as the Priest's House. The Mexicans had fortified the building and now they brought up cannon to defend it. Just before midnight the Texians attacked, crowbars slashing, rifles cracking, and bowie knives at the ready. The Mexican defenders fought valiantly, but could not resist the fever of the Texian onslaught. They finally retreated to the church.

General Cós knew that all was lost. He could retreat across the river to the Alamo, but the mission-turned-garrison was already crowded with troops and refugees from the city, and the arrival of the 600 convict soldiers had filled it to overflowing. Food supplies were very low. The 600 were of no use; most of them could not even load a cannon. The next Texian attack would be at the center of resistance, the plaza, and once that fell the Texians would turn the cannon on the Alamo.

Early on December 9, Cós called his officers together. First he asked a question of his adjutant, José Juan Sánchez Navarro. Had the rebels occupied the plaza?

No. It was still defended by about seventy regulars under Col. Nicolas Condelle.

Seventy men! That meant the plaza would soon be lost. Cós's mind was made up.

"Sánchez," he said, no trace of the bravado of *Deguello* in his voice, "by reason of cowardice and the perfidy of some, many of our comrades are lost. Go and save those brave men. I authorize you to approach the enemy and obtain the best terms possible. Save the dignity of our government, the honor of its army, and the honor of life and property of the troops that still remain, even though I, myself, shall perish."

At the Alamo, the *Deguello* flag was lowered and the eagle and serpent flag of Mexico was replaced by a white banner. Sánchez Navarro led a three-man delegation toward the Texian position under a white flag. The mission was stopped by Colonel Condelle, commander of the Morelos battalion.

"You may not pass," the colonel said. "The Morelos battalion has not given up. We are still fighting."

It took a lot of convincing by Sánchez Navarro to persuade the colonel that the orders came from General Cós. By the time he did, the rebels were waiting for them. They had just buried Ben Milam, the first fallen hero of the revolution. General Burleson appeared from headquarters and began negotiations, which lasted until two o'clock in the morning. The gentleman Mexican officers were appalled by the appearance of the Texians, in their rough buckskins and boots, donning the silver spurs and other finery they had stripped from dead Mexican soldiers. "Crude bumpkins, proud and overbearing" was how Colonel Sánchez Navarro described them.

But a peace treaty was arranged. The seven-week siege of San Antonio de Béxar was over. At ten o'clock on the morning of December 10, 1835, the treaty was signed in the Martinez house, which would later be called the Cós house. On December 13 General Cós led his army of 1,100 men out of San Antonio toward the Rio Grande.

The Texian Army was disbanded, and the volunteers went home for Christmas with no intention of coming back. The San Antonio Greys moved into the Alamo, occupying the chapel, cooking up their beef and venison over open fires, and hanging around, waiting for excitement. The women of San Antonio came back to the Alamo, crossing the little wooden bridge over the San Antonio River to come and pray at the carved sandstone statues of St. Francis and St. Dominic that occupied the niches of the chapel. Although they ostentatiously ignored the young soldiers, some of the Greys cast admiring glances in the direction of the young *señoritas.*

Boredom set in quickly. These men had come to Texas looking for war and glory, and it seemed that it was all over. General Houston knew better. He knew that the Mexicans had not yet begun to fight. To placate the Greys and encourage other Americans, he revived the plan for an attack on Matamoros. He wrote Jim Bowie, ordering him to lead the expedition and then to hold the port of Copano on the Brazos. New volunteers were to report there. Bowie was supposed to be in San Felipe, but when Houston's letter arrived he had gone back to San Antonio and never received the letter. Meanwhile a certain confusion reigned. Dr. Grant and Frank Johnson picked up their plans for the Matamoros Expedition, then stripped the garrisons of San Antonio and Goliad of supplies

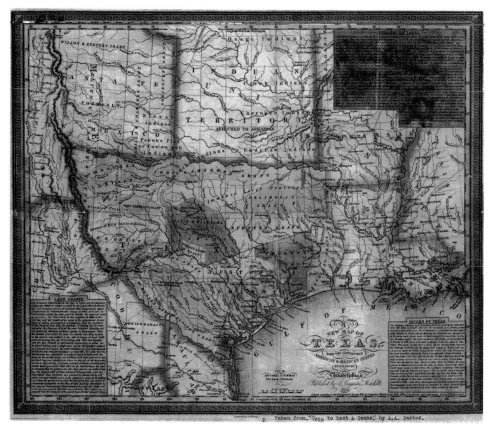

THIS 1835 MAP OF TEXAS WITH THE SURROUNDING AMERICAN AND MEXICAN
STATES INCLUDES SUCH FEATURES AS THE OLD SAN ANTONIO ROAD AND THE
GREAT SPANISH ROAD TO RED RIVER.
TEXAS STATE LIBRARY & ARCHIVES COMMISSION

and horses, taking even the clothes of the garrison soldiers. Colonel Neill,
assigned by Sam Houston in late December to command the post at San
Antonio, was left with a skeleton garrison and only eighty men to defend it.

Still, the Texians were ecstatic in their hard-won victory. They had lost Ben
Milam and sixteen others, dead or wounded, but the Mexicans had suffered at
least 150 casualties. Governor Smith and the council agreed that the Texians and
Tejanos were "the invincible brave sons of freedom"—but the governor and the
council could agree on nothing else. San Felipe was a forest of confusion where
insane ideas flourished.

To add to the confusion, from Stephen Austin in New Orleans came a letter recommending that Texas declare her independence from Mexico. "The uni-
versal wish and expectation in this quarter," he said, "is that Texas ought to
declare herself independent at once."

SEVEN

❧

The Defense of
the Alamo

The defeat of General Cós in December 1835 angered Santa
Anna, and the reason for this was that it upset his timetable. He had intended to
deal with Texas in the spring of 1836, but this was an emergency; the immigrants
had shown their perfidious designs and they would be brought to book. If they
wanted blood, he would give them blood; the suppression of Zacatecas would
look like a picnic.

Santa Anna promised that the year 1836 would see the destruction of those
who wanted to divide Mexico.

The nucleus of the force to be sent to Texas would be the Army of
Zacatecas. *El Presidente* did not expect much trouble in suppressing this rebel-
lion and bringing centralization to all of Mexico. Minister of War José María
Tornel put it succinctly:

The superiority of the Mexican soldier over the mountaineers of
Kentucky and the hunters of Missouri is well known. Veterans seasoned by twenty years of wars can't be intimidated by the presence of

José Urrea
1795=1849

José Urrea was born in Tucson, in what is now Arizona, but his family roots were in Durango, Mexico. Urrea called himself a *criollo* although he was really a *mestizo* (half Spanish, half Indian). He entered the Spanish Royal Army when he was twelve years old, and his early career was spent in suppressing revolutionary outbreaks.

In 1824 he was promoted to captain because of his successes, but he soon left the Army to tend to his family estates in Durango. When the Spanish came again in 1829, Urrea rejoined the army as a major. He liberated Durango for Santa Anna, who was still posing as a liberal; when Santa Anna became President, Urrea was promoted to colonel. Urrea was a reluctant participant in the suppression of Zacatecas in 1834, then was promoted to Brigadier General and sent to Durango to fight Apaches.

In 1835 Santa Anna called Urrea to join the army bound for Texas. He defeated the rebels at San Patricio, Refugio, Goliad, and Coleto Creek, where Fannin's column surrendered. Urrea did not like Santa Anna's No Quarter policy and specifically objected to the massacre of the prisoners of Goliad. Here Urrea was overruled by Santa Anna, who later tried to blame Urrea for the slaughter.

Santa Anna wanted to go back to Mexico City after the Alamo was retaken. Only because General Urrea was conducting a successful series of battles and stealing Santa Anna's thunder did the dictator decide to resume command of operations in the spring of 1836. After Santa Anna was defeated at San Jacinto and ordered General Filisola to evacuate Texas, General Urrea tried unsuccessfully to persuade Filisola to ignore the order, a move which was clearly illegal as Santa Anna was a prisoner of war and under duress. Later General Filisola was court-martialed for this act.

A strong anti-Centralist, Urrea fell out with Santa Anna in 1837 and joined the resistance against him, but was defeated in battle at Mazatlan in 1838. He then attempted a failed coup at Tampico and was imprisoned, escaping several times only to be captured again.

He was returned to duty during the brief war with France, but when Anastasio Bustamante came to power in 1840, Urrea led another uprising that failed. He fled home to Durango and there raised an army in the Federalist cause, which Santa Anna once again agreed to espouse. During the Mexican-American War, Urrea commanded a cavalry division, and shortly after the war's end, he died of cholera.

A determined Federalist and a successful governor and senator of Durango, Urrea was also a thoroughly competent professional soldier. If Santa Anna had taken his military advice, Texas might still be part of Mexico.

an army ignorant of the art of war, incapable of discipline, and renowned for insubordination.

At the end of 1835, the Army of Zacatecas, which was now called the Army of Operations (in Texas), assembled at San Luis Potosí and then moved to Saltillo. In mid-January 1836, General Cós came dragging in with his defeated army of 1,100. Santa Anna lectured his brother-in-law, told him not to be a fool and keep his promise not to fight the Texians again, and ordered him to rest his troops and then join the army of 6,000 that would invade Texas.

It would be a pincers operation, involving a main force under Santa Anna and a mobile force under Gen. José Urrea. Santa Anna would take El Camino Réal across the Northern Mexico desert, through the plains and mountains of Coahuila. Urrea would branch off at Matamoros, cross the Rio Grande, and then sweep along the coastal plain to Goliad. Generals Filisola, Sesma, and Cós would march to San Antonio. Santa Anna would personally lead the attack on Goliad or San Antonio, depending on the circumstances. He had chosen Goliad and San Antonio because it was said "he who controls Goliad and Béxar has Texas in the palm of his hand."

After training and supply-gathering, the army moved out: General Urrea first, then the main corps, two infantry brigades, Gen. Asesma Andrade's cavalry,

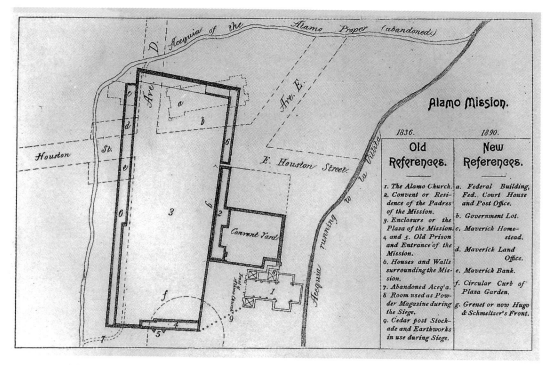

THIS PLAN OF THE ALAMO COMPARES THE 1836 SITE TO THAT OF 1890. IT
APPEARED IN *SAN ANTONIO DE BEXAR: A GUIDE & HISTORY.*
TEXAS STATE LIBRARY & ARCHIVES COMMISSION

and Santa Anna with his personal cavalry guard. In the first week of February they
reached Monclova, where they picked up General Filisola. They marched again,
an impressive army of four thousand men and twelve cannon, the infantry men in
their tall shakos and bright uniforms. The main column strung on for miles.

The march across the northern desert was dangerous and exhausting. It was
the depth of the coldest winter in many years. The soldiers were on short
rations: eight ounces of hardtack a day. They froze, and some died. They
wrapped their feet in rags; they were hungry, and ate mesquite nuts, rats, chip-
munks, and maguey to supplement their diet; but somehow most of the men
survived. One night, a blue norther dumped fifteen inches of snow on the
ground. Another night, General Urrea lost six of his soldiers—Mayan Indians
from the tropical district of Yucatán—to exposure.

The army left a trail of dead animals and broken equipment scattered along
its route, but on February 12, Santa Anna and his army reached the shore of the
Rio Grande. Texas spread before them. Four days later, after much-needed rest,
the main force crossed the river.

At the beginning of February, the Texas Army was in disarray. General

David (Davy) Crockett
1786–1836

Long before the Battle of the Alamo, Davy Crockett was famous as a hunter, frontiersman, writer, and orator. It is said that when he was a Tennessee state representative, he killed 108 bears between two sessions of the legislature. This tale may be apocryphal, but many people believed it because Crockett's larger-than-life character was so well established.

Born on August 17, 1786, in what is now northeastern Tennessee, Crockett spent much of his farm-boy youth in the woods. By the time he was thirteen he was totally self-reliant, but he did not learn to read and write until he was eighteen, when he went to school to impress a girl. When she jilted him after six months, he left school and soon thereafter married, began farming, and raised a family.

Crockett volunteered for Andrew Jackson's army in the Creek War, but soon grew disgusted with American treatment of the Indians and hired a substitute to finish his enlistment. His wife bore three children but died in 1815, and he later married a widow with two children. Despite his lack of formal education, Crockett was chosen as magistrate in his local community. He was always proud of the fact that, although he had no legal training, none of his decisions as a judge was ever overturned. In 1821 and again in 1823 he was elected to the Tennessee legislature, and when the house was not in session he went hunting—thus the story of the bears. In 1828 Crockett was elected to Congress and served until 1833, when he was defeated for reelection after he quarreled with President Andrew Jackson over relocation of Indians.

Disgusted with politics, he made a triumphal tour of the major cities of the East, where the name Davy Crockett was well known for his writings. He grew interested in Texas and decided to go there, leaving Tennessee with

DAVY CROCKETT IN 1834, FROM A PAINTING BY SAMUEL STILLMAN OSGOOD. TENNESSE STATE LIBRARY

a typical statement to constituents: "You may all go to Hell and I will go to Texas."

In the fall of 1835 he arrived in Texas with his fiddle and a dozen adherents, members of his personal rifleman company. In January 1836 he wrote to one of his stepdaughters back in Tennessee, "I would rather be in my present situation than be elected to a seat in Congress for life." A few weeks later he was in the Alamo, fighting for Texas Independence. One story says that he fell on the firing line while another, by Mexican Lieutenant de la Peña, says Davy Crockett tried to surrender along with five others but was put to death by Santa Anna's order. The heroic death story, supported by Alamo survivor Susannah Dickinson, is much more in character.

Houston was off making peace with the Cherokee and did not know that Colonel Bowie and Colonel Neill had defied his orders against defending the Alamo. On February 3, Colonel Travis and thirty men arrived to bolster the Alamo defense. Four days later, Davy Crockett and his contingent of twelve Tennesseeans came in. They were accompanied by John McGregor, a colonist from Scotland, whom they had met at Nacogdoches. McGregor had flaming red hair and a set of bagpipes, both of which endeared him to the Tennesseeans.

Davy Crockett was famous, a well-known writer, politician, and orator. He was forty-nine years old and had lived an adventurous life; he had been a backwoods hunter, soldier in the Creek War, and congressman from Tennessee. After he was defeated for reelection to Congress in 1835, he came to Texas for a change of scene. He arrived at Nacogdoches in early January and joined the Volunteer Auxiliary Corps of Texas on January 14 as a private. With him came a contingent of twelve Tennessee riflemen, who also joined the Alamo defense.

As Jim Bowie and Colonel Neill bolstered the Alamo defenses, Colonel Johnson and Dr. Grant were busily moving toward the invasion of Matamoros.

On February 4, 1836, Colonel Fannin landed his 450 men at Copano and marched twenty-five miles inland to Refugio, the kickoff point for the Matamoros invasion. When he got there, he learned that General Urrea was in Matamoros, preparing to cross the Rio Grande. Fannin, not wanting to be caught, left Refugio and marched twenty-five miles northwest to Goliad.

In San Antonio on February 11, Colonel Neill learned that his wife and children were ill at home. He took home leave to join them. Before he left, he appointed Colonel Travis to be temporary commander of the Alamo garrison, but the volunteer troops objected and voted Colonel Bowie into the job. It was agreed then that Bowie would command the volunteers and Travis would command the regulars. Neill would return as soon as possible with provisions and medical supplies.

The shared leadership was difficult for both men. Bowie issued orders without consulting Travis; he stopped the exit of carts from San Antonio because the people were taking away food. He declared that all the food was needed for defense. He ordered the jails opened and the convicts released so they could fight for the defense. (Antonio Fuentes was one of the released convicts who elected to join the Alamo garrison.) Travis complained about Bowie's drinking and high-handed manner, and threatened to send the regular troops out of town.

However, Bowie was ill with typhoid fever and found it increasingly necessary to depend on Travis. In time, Travis and Bowie reconciled. Travis then supervised the buildup of the Alamo defenses. Chief Engineer Green Jameson and Capt. Almeron Dickinson, the artillery officer, sited more of the guns captured from the Cós army in December. Hiram Williamson, a young Philadelphian just fresh from West Point, was appointed sergeant major and began a course of drill that most of the volunteers cheerfully accepted. Part of

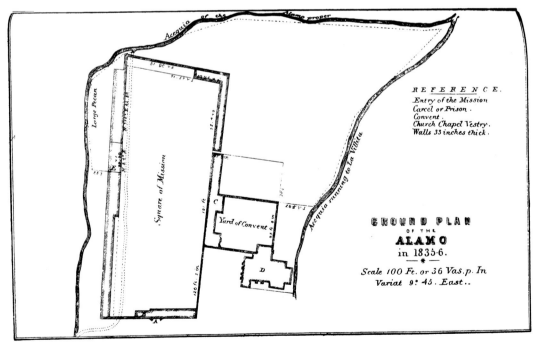

THIS MAP FROM HENDERSON YOAKUM'S *HISTORY OF TEXAS* SHOWS THE ALAMO'S GROUND PLAN AT THE TIME OF ITS FAMOUS SEIGE.

DR. AMOS POLLARD, CHIEF SURGEON OF THE ALAMO GARRISON. PAINTING BY AMELIA WILLIAMS.
TEXAS STATE LIBRARY & ARCHIVES COMMISSION

one company of the New Orleans Greys opted out of the Matamoros Expedition and changed their name to the San Antonio Greys. They practiced drilling along with the rest.

Meanwhile, Dr. Amos Pollard established a hospital in several of the rooms of the old barracks. Engineer Jameson and Captain Dickinson, the artillery officer, sited cannon, and breastworks were erected; the guns here were mounted on platforms and fired over the wall.

The Tejanos were in the thick of it. Juan Seguín sent his nephew Blas Herrera to Laredo to spy on the Mexican army. Herrera was an experienced scout. He and his Indian assistants saw the columns of Mexican troops cross the Rio Grande. They followed, and each night assassinated sentries and escaped in the darkness. They destroyed bridges and harried the Mexicans on the march. Herrera returned to San Antonio in mid-February to report to Juan Seguín a large force of Mexican soldiers crossing the Rio Grande. Seguín reported this to Travis, who brought Herrera before the Texian leaders at the Alamo. They listened to his story suspiciously. Finally one of them interrupted.

"Crazy Mexican," he said. "You're drunk!"

Insulted, Herrera stormed off. Seguín followed him. But Travis reconsidered, and dispatched Herrera to carry the news to General Houston. When Herrera arrived he was detained by Houston, who wanted his services as scout.

Most of the *norteamericanos* snorted and said it was a trumped-up story, more Mexican lies, but on February 23, the first Mexican troops appeared, two battalions of the dragoon regiment of Dolores to take possession of San Antonio. The Texian and Tejano members of the garrison hastily moved to the Alamo that day, and several Tejano families followed, carrying their possessions over the footbridge to the fortress, past the Mexican soldiers riding into the plaza. Colonel Travis also immediately sent a messenger asking for help to Colonel Fannin in Goliad.

The preparations continued, and more women and children came in. Susannah Dickinson, the wife of the artillery captain, had arrived from Gonzales, where she had been forced out of her house by looters who knew that her husband was in San Antonio. She and her daughter moved into the Alamo. The women and children clustered in the chapel while their men prepared to man the guns and fight.

The Mexican cavalry's possession of the city was signaled by the firing of a field piece from the military plaza and the rasing of the *Deguello* flag over the church. Mexican officers soon appeared with a white flag on the footbridge. Capt. Albert Martin led a Texian delegation to the bridge. The Mexican officers presented them with a letter from Col. Juan Almonte, General Santa Anna's aide and interpreter, demanding immediate and unconditional surrender of the Alamo. Martin said they would report the demand to Colonel Travis. They crossed back over the bridge and gave the letter to Travis. The eighteen-pounder was fired in reply.

The siege of the Alamo had begun.

EIGHT

The Coming of Santa Anna

On the morning of February 23, General Santa Anna had arrived. He handed his horse to a soldier and climbed the tower of the church of San Fernando, the highest building in town. He looked across the river at the Alamo; there the flag of the defenders waved provocatively. He came down and immediately ordered that the blood-red *Deguello* flag be flown from the church. To that provocation, the Texians answered the demand to surrender with a cannon shot.

So the rules were established. The Texas men would not surrender. When the Alamo fell, any survivors would be put to the sword.

Santa Anna's arrival had come as a complete surprise to the Texians. The city streets swarmed with people fleeing in all directions. The Mexican soldiers took their time coming in—it was an hour more before there was any appreciable group in town. Meanwhile, the last men of the garrison gathered their belongings and hastened to the fort. In an hour San Antonio was quiet again, but had the Mexican soldiers hastened they might have captured the Alamo without a fight. Later Santa Anna said that if his soldiers had not dawdled while breaking camp that morning, he would have been spared a lot of trouble. That's how great a surprise the arrival of the Mexican Army was.

When Colonel Travis saw the *Deguello* flag flying from the church belfry he had ordered a shot fired from the eighteen-pounder, the largest of his twenty guns. Having shown his defiance, Travis hastened to send a courier to Fannin at Goliad with the message: "We hope you will send us all the men you can spare promptly. We have one hundred and fory-six men, who are determined never to retreat."

Help was coming from America, but it could not possibly arrive in time to save the Alamo. The only hope lay within the Texas colonies, and by far the largest contingent of armed men was under Fannin's command. If no help came Travis would have to fight the Mexicans on their own terms.

Jim Bowie asked Travis if he had heard a Mexican bugle blowing just before he had ordered the firing of the shot of defiance. In the excitement of the moment, Travis had not heard the bugle call to parley issued by the Mexicans.

The *Deguello* flag was hung up there as a warning, not a threat, said Bowie. Why had Travis fired the cannon?

The conversation was punctuated by the explosion of four seven-inch howitzer bombs in the Alamo plaza. No one was hurt, but Bowie's point was emphasized.

Bowie sent Green Jameson out to cross the river with a white flag and a message. The message, written in Bowie's excellent Spanish, said that the cannon had been fired before the bugle was blown and the Texians were ready to parley. But Santa Anna had been angered; the reply brought back by Jameson was that Santa Anna would accept nothing but surrender at discretion— Unconditional Surrender.

This attempt to negotiate was Bowie's last gesture of leadership. His condition worsened overnight, and he took to his bed with a high fever. The next morning, he turned complete command of the garrison over to Travis.

Bowie had brought into The Alamo for protection two relatives (by marriage): Juana Alsbury, adopted daughter of Governor Veramendi, and her sister Gertrudis Navarro. Knowing that typhoid fever was infectious, he had himself moved from the part of the building occupied by Mrs. Alsbury and her sister to a little room at one side of the hospital, near the entrance. Two soldiers came to carry him away. On leaving, he spoke to Mrs. Alsbury.

"Sister, do not be afraid," he said. "I leave you with Colonel Travis, Colonel Crockett, and other friends. They are gentlemen and they will treat you kindly."

THESE THREE OLD MEN WERE ONCE YOUNG AND VIGOROUS COURIERS OF THE ALAMO IN FEBRUARY 1836. BENJAMIN HIGHSMITH, DR. JOHN SUTHERLAND, AND WILLIAM S. OURY (*CLOCKWISE FROM UPPER LEFT*) SURVIVED THE FALL OF THE ALAMO BY BRAVING THE DANGERS OF THE MEXICAN SIEGE TO CARRY MESSAGES FOR HELP TO VARIOUS TEXIAN COMMUNITIES.

TEXAS STATE LIBRARY & ARCHIVES COMMISSION; CENTER FOR AMERICAN HISTORY, UNIVERSITY OF TEXAS AT AUSTIN; ARIZONA HISTORICAL SOCIETY, TUCSON

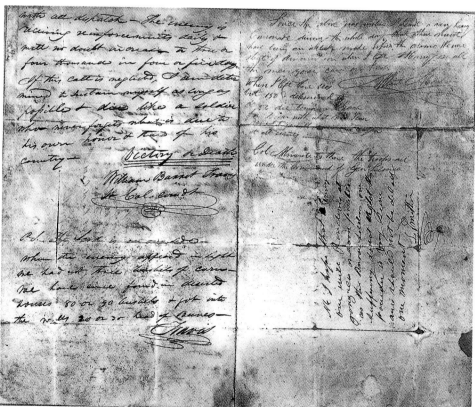

FACSIMILE OF COLONEL TRAVIS'S LETTER OF FEBRUARY 24, 1836, ANNOUNCING
THE MEXICAN SIEGE OF THE ALAMO. ADDITIONAL REMARKS BY COURIER ALBERT
MARTIN APPEAR ON THE LAST PAGE.

TEXAS STATE LIBRARY & ARCHIVES COMMISSION

Travis was a busy man then; he was still organizing the defenses, but he was also writing letters furiously and sending out couriers to beg for assistance. He was also very concerned about supplies. That night he sent men out to forage in La Villita, a shanty town just southwest of the Alamo walls. They came back with eighty bushels of corn and beans and thirty head of cattle. The Mexicans were besieging the Alamo, but the siege was less than tight. As a matter of fact, Texians would slip through the Mexican lines almost daily until the day of the final attack.

Santa Anna spent the rest of February 23 sending messages to his straggling commands, demanding that they catch up. He particularly wanted the twelve-pound cannon. He did not want to attack without them, but they were far behind, so the next few days were spent waiting. The Mexicans kept up a harassing fire all day, and the Texians returned it. It was the lull before the storm.

The first two Mexican batteries arrived on February 24 and were placed about 1,000 feet from the Alamo. Each battery consisted of four guns, though the twelve-pounders were still on the road.

That day, Colonel Travis wrote a message addressed "To the People of Texas and all Americans *in the World—*"

Fellow citizens and compatriots—

I am besieged, by a thousand or more of the Mexicans under Santa Anna—I have sustained a continual Bombardment & cannonade for 24 hours & have not lost a man—The enemy has demanded a surrender at discretion, otherwise, the garrison are to be put to the sword, if the fort is taken—I have answered the demand with a cannon shot, & our flag still waves proudly from the walls—*I shall never surrender or retreat. Then,* I call on you in the name of Liberty, of patriotism && every thing dear to the American character, to come to our aid, with all dispatch—The enemy is receiving reinforcements daily & will no doubt increase to three or four thousand in four or five days. If this call is neglected, I am determined to sustain myself as long as possible & die like a soldier who never forgets what is due to his own honor & that of his country—

VICTORY OR DEATH

William Barret Travis
Lt. Col. Comdt.

Lorenzo de Zavala
1789≠1836

Lorenzo de Zavala came from a wealthy Yucatán family and was trained as a doctor, but in his twenties he went into politics. He was elected to the Spanish Cortés (Parliament) in 1814, but en route to Madrid he was arrested and imprisoned by order of the king because of his liberal sentiments. He remained in prison on an island off Vera Cruz for three years.

After his release from prison, he practiced medicine for a while and spent some time in Spain, then joined the Mexican Constituent Assembly that drew up the liberal Constitution of 1824. He was deeply involved in the political infighting of Mexico in the 1820s. His connection with Texas began in 1829, when he received a grant to settle 500 families.

Although he did not immediately take up the role of *empresario,* his involvement in politics drove him into exile for three years. He returned to Mexico in 1832, and the next year became Minister to France in the first Santa Anna administration. He broke with Santa Anna over the issue of centralism of power, went to Texas, and became a political force there.

LORENZO DE ZAVALA, VICE PRESIDENT OF THE TEXAS PROVISIONAL GOVERNMENT. HE SERVED VERY BRIEFLY BEFORE HE WAS TAKEN ILL.
TEXAS STATE LIBRARY & ARCHIVES COMMISSION

De Zavala was a signer of the Texas Declaration of Independence in 1835 and was elected vice president of the provisional government of the republic, but resigned shortly after because of ill health. He died in the autumn of 1836. He was a proud intellectual and a historian, and he had the honor of being selected by Santa Anna as his worst enemy. The president of Mexico often spoke of hanging Zavala higher than all the rest of the rebels.

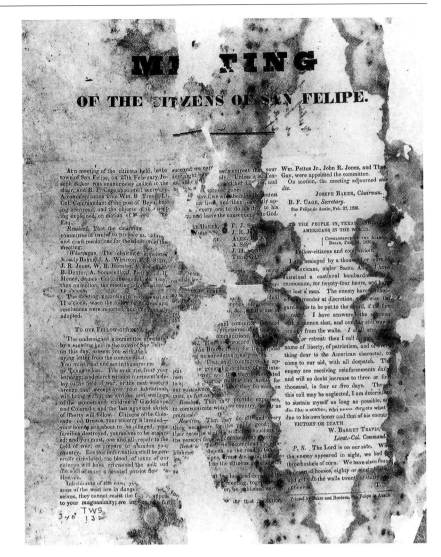

A BROADSIDE
REPORTING ON A
MEETING OF THE
CITIZENS OF SAN
FELIPE ON
FEBRUARY 27,
1836, INCLUDING
THE FAMOUS LET-
TER FROM
COLONEL TRAVIS
ANNOUNCING THE
SIEGE.
*TEXAS STATE
LIBRARY &
ARCHIVES
COMMISSION*

After writing this message and dispatching the courier, Albert Martin, he lay down his pen and picked up a rifle.

On the morning of February 25, 200 Mexican infantry suddenly appeared on the edge of La Villita, organized a skirmish line, and began an attack. In the Alamo, the soldiers fired back with everything they had—rifles, muskets, shotguns, cannon, and even pistols. The line wavered and broke, and the attack fizzled out. But Travis decided to act before they could repeat the performance. That night he sent raiders out to La Villita to burn the shanty town to the ground. About three hundred Mexican infantrymen appeared and a firefight followed, the Texians covered by riflemen from the fort. At about one o'clock a cold rain began to fall on San Antonio and the fierce battle ended. Everyone knew what was coming next: A blue norther was about to strike, a meteorological disturbance caused by a cold front sweeping down across the Texas plain from Canada. In a blue norther, the temperature could drop thirty degrees in an hour. The effect was intensified by the wind-chill factor. Santa Anna's army had already been through two of these storms and had lost horses and men to them.

The weather turned intensely cold. The men shivered around their fires and huddled in their ponchos to try to keep warm. To divert the Mexican soldiers, the regimental bands played marches and folk music that was also enjoyed by the Texians. Members of the garrison unlimbered their own instruments—guitars, mouth organs, and the like. Davy Crockett got out his fiddle. The Scotsman John McGregor got out his bagpipes, and they staged a spirited test to see who could make the most noise. The contest proved so popular that they repeated it every night around the campfires.

Colonel Travis was still hoping for reinforcement, still concerned with the greater struggle. He wrote a friend that he hoped the convention in Washington-on-the-Brazos would declare independence. On the night of February 25, he sent Juan Seguín to General Houston with an appeal. Seguín's horse had gone lame, so he asked Jim Bowie for his. Bowie was so sick he could hardly see, but he lent Seguín his horse. Accompanied by Antonio Cruz Rocha, the captain started out from the Alamo. They made their way under cover of the burning La Villita. Once clear, they headed up the Gonzales road.

A few miles further on they encountered a Mexican roadblock. The cavalrymen were dismounted, standing around a fire. When the two riders approached someone challenged:

"Quién está?"

In his native Spanish, Juan Seguín responded. The questioner thought he was a Mexican army officer. When they got near the pile of brush that was the roadblock, they spurred their horses and leaped clear. Shots rang out and the cavalrymen gave chase, but they did not catch the couriers. The message to General Houston was delivered.

Santa Anna received more reinforcements on February 26 and a battery of artillery was erected northeast of the Alamo. Some Texians sallied forth and burned some houses 800 yards away, and another party drove off the Mexican cavalry attempting to circle around to the rear of the Alamo.

Travis's appeal to Fannin arrived at Goliad on the morning of February 26. Fannin had sent James Bonham back a few days before with excuses, but this time he read the desperation in Travis's words and ordered his troops to march. He had more than 300 men and four field guns, but little ammunition and so few horses that he had to use oxen to draw the wagons.

On the 27th, the Mexicans sent an officer to the Seguín farm to search for grain, cattle, and hogs. The decision was made that day to cut off the water supply of the Alamo and the ditch was blocked. Enrique Esparza was walking through the Alamo plaza that evening and heard Antonio Fuentes, another of Seguín's men, talking to another soldier. "Did you hear that they have cut the water off?" the soldier asked. Fuentes reassured him. He knew that the defenders still had the well inside the compound.

The Mexicans tried to put a new bridge across the river near the Alamo, but the Texas riflemen shot down thirty of them. The engineers ceased. That night, Santa Anna sent a message to Mexico City by courier, announcing the capture of San Antonio.

None of this was known to Fannin as he prepared to go to the aid of the Alamo. He marched on February 28. Within two hours, three wagons broke down, and when the column reached the ford across the San Antonio River the oxen could not drag the artillery across. The river was too badly swollen from the rains. Manhandling the equipment across took all afternoon. Once across, the men found they had guns but no ammunition, for the ammunition wagons were on the other side of the river. The force was stuck; they had traveled about a half a mile. No one guarded or tethered the livestock that night, and the next morning they found that the oxen and horses had wandered off and had to be rounded up before they could move.

Colonel Fannin called a council of officers. As they were meeting, a courier came from Goliad bearing the message that a load of supplies had reached Matagordo, where it lay unguarded. Fannin decided to go back to Goliad and then go after the supplies.

Fannin received more messages from Travis, but he did not reply. One of those messages said that Travis would fire the eighteen-pounder three times a day, morning, noon, and evening, to show that the Alamo still held out.

At San Antonio, General Santa Anna proved to be the best scout of his army. He was constantly on the move, reconnoitering and moving troops from this side to that. On the night of February 29, he sent General Sesma's cavalry along the road to Goliad. He had the correct intelligence that Fannin's force was coming. But Sesma found nothing, and sent a message to Santa Anna from the old Mission de la Spada saying just that early on the morning of March 1. He then brought his troops back to San Antonio.

That afternoon was a busy one for the defenders of the Alamo. They fired a twelve-pound cannon at the Iturbi house, which was occupied by Santa Anna, and scored several hits, but no casualties. After midnight John Smith arrived

COL. JAMES BONHAM, COMMANDER OF THE MOBILE GREYS, LATER COURIER FOR COLONEL TRAVIS, WHO DIED AT THE ALAMO MANNING A CANNON ON MARCH 6, 1836. THIS PAINTING IS BY CHARLES B. NORMANN. *TEXAS STATE LIBRARY & ARCHIVES COMMISSION*

from Gonzales with thirty-two volunteers who had decided to join the Alamo defense. These were members of the Gonzales Ranging Company of Mounted Volunteers. They included settlers like George Washington Cottle, who had a wife and children in Gonzales, and Marcus L. Sewell, who was just fresh off the boat from England. The thirty-two arrived unscathed until they reached the Alamo walls, where one was shot in the foot by a trigger-happy Texian. The wounded man let out a mighty oath in English, and there was no more firing as they rode through the gate.

But these were the last of the reinforcements, save one. James Bonham, acting as a courier, went to Goliad, where he met Fannin's returning relief force. He tried to convince Fannin to make another attempt. Fannin tried to persuade

TEXAS

EXPECTS EVERY MAN TO DO HIS DUTY.

{ EXECUTIVE DEPARTMENT
OF TEXAS.

FELLOW-CITIZENS OF TEXAS,

The enemy are upon us! A strong force surrounds the walls of San Antonio, and threaten that Garrison with the sword. Our country imperiously demands the service of every patriotic arm, and longer to continue in a state of *apathy* will be *criminal.* Citizens of Texas, descendants of Washington, awake! arouse yourselves!! The question is now to be decided, are we to continue as freemen, or bow beneath the rod of military despotism. Shall we, without a struggle, sacrifice our fortunes, our lives and our liberties, or shall we imitate the example of our forefathers, and hurl destruction upon the hands of our oppressors? The eyes of the world are upon us! All friends of liberty and of the rights of men, are anxious spectators of our conflict; or deeply enlisted in our cause. Shall we disappoint their hopes and expectations? No; let us at once fly to our arms, march to the battle field, meet the foe, and give renewed evidence to the world, that the arms of freemen, uplifted in defence of their rights and liberties, are irresistible. "Now is the day and now is the hour," that Texas expects every man to do his duty. Let us shew ourselves worthy to be free, *and we shall be free.* Our brethren of the United States have, with a generosity and a devotion to liberty, unparalleled in the annals of men, offered us every assistance. We have arms, ammunition, clothing and provisions; all we have to do, is to sustain ourselves for the present. Rest assured that succors will reach us,' and that the people of the United States will not permit the chains of slavery to be rivetted on us.

Fellow-Citizens, your garrison at San Antonio is surrounded by more than twenty times their numbers. Will you see them perish by the hands of a mercenary soldiery, without an effort for their relief? They cannot sustain the seige more than thirty days; for the sake of humanity, before that time give them succor. Citizens of the east, your brethren of the Brazos and Colorado, expect your assistance, afford it, and check the march of the enemy and suffer not your own land to become the seat of war; without your immediate aid we cannot sustain the war. Fellow-citizens, I call upon you as your executive officer to "turn out;" it is your country that demands your help. He who longer slumbers on the volcano, must be a madman. He who refuses to aid his country in this, her hour of peril and danger is a traitor. All persons able to bear arms in Texas are called on to rendezvous at the town of Gonzales, with the least possible delay armed and equipped for battle. *Our rights and liberties must be protected*; to the battle field march and save the country. An approving world smiles upon us, the God of battles is on our side, and victory awaits us.

Confidently believing that your energies will be sufficient for the occasion, and that your efforts will be ultimately successful.

I subscribe myself your fellow-citizen,

HENRY SMITH,
Governor.

PROCLAMATION OF GOV. HENRY SMITH FROM FEBRUARY 1836 CALLING TEXIANS TO ARMS TO DEFEND THE ALAMO, "TO RENDEZVOUS AT THE TOWN OF GONZALES, WITH THE LEAST POSSIBLE DELAY ARMED AND EQUIPPED FOR BATTLE." *TEXAS STATE LIBRARY & ARCHIVES COMMISSION*

Bonham not to go back to the Alamo. It would mean certain death, he said.

Bonham spat on the ground and said Travis deserved a reply at least. He left Goliad, rode hard, and reached the Alamo on the morning of March 3. He gave Travis the bad news about the failed expedition. Now Travis knew there would be no more help.

Juan Nepomuceno Almonte
1803–1869

Juan Almonte was General Santa Anna's aide and interpreter. Present at the siege and storming of the Alamo and at the Battle of San Jacinto, he interpreted the conversations between General Sam Houston and Santa Anna regarding the Mexican surrender.

The son of a Mexican revolutionary war hero, Almonte was educated in the United States. There he learned to speak colloquial American English, which allowed him to dupe the Texas ferryman when Santa Anna wanted to cross the Brazos. The Santa Anna party hid in the bushes on the riverbank while Almonte called the ferryman. Thinking Almonte was a Texian officer, the ferryman came and was captured, giving Santa Anna his transport.

In the 1840s Almonte was Mexican Minister to Washington and announced the breaking of diplomatic relations following the American annexation of Texas in 1845— Mexico still claimed Texas as part of a Mexican province. He served as president of Mexico for six months in 1862 after Benito Juarez was ousted. Almonte was instrumental in engineering the French intervention in Mexico in 1861 and became a major general in Emperor Maximilian's army. He died in exile in Paris.

COL. JUAN N. ALMONTE.
UT INSTITUTE OF TEXAN CULTURES AT SAN ANTONIO

NINE

~

Waiting

Mexican Lieutenant Menchard had not found any food at the Juan Seguín farm on February 27, but on March 2 he was sent back. Santa Anna insisted there was food there. Santa Anna was not only his own best scout, he was a superior intelligence officer. That day he discovered a covered road within pistol shot of the Alamo and posted the Jimenez battalion there.

In someone else's army he might have been a big success. What he lacked were real qualities of leadership.

General Castrillón would put it clearly to Col. Pedro Delgado on the eve of the Battle of San Jacinto seven weeks later. Delgado was concerned about the site Santa Anna had chosen for the Mexican camp; he went to Castrillón as the senior general and found him standing outside Santa Anna's tent.

"What can I do, my friend?" the general said in caustic tones loud enough to be heard inside the tent. "You know that nothing avails here against the caprice, arbitrary will, and ignorance of that man."

Now, on the afternoon of March 2, there was a lull in the firing. The defenders of the Alamo were aroused by the sound of cheering coming from the city. They rushed to the walls and the gun platforms and the church and saw people swarming in the streets, shouting and waving:

"Santa Anna, Santa Anna," was the cry.

More than 1,000 soldiers came marching from the west. Gen. Antonio

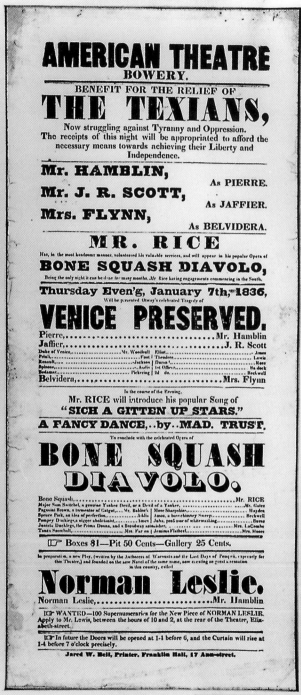

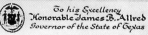

Gaona's troops had arrived. The only element missing was the twelve-pound cannon, though Gaona brought ten lesser guns. This gave Santa Anna something specific to do. He spent the afternoon siting guns, ordering trenches dug, and in general showing off to his officers.

More good news for the Mexican Army that afternoon: A courier arrived with a report of General Urrea's victory at San Patricio. The bells of San Fernando Church pealed, and a surge of optimism swelled through the Mexican camp. After weeks of bad news, the tide seemed to have turned. Colonel Almonte was elated. He wrote his sister in Mexico City, asking that his mail be forwarded to San Antonio, for it looked as though the campaign would soon be over and he would be there for a while.

Jim Bowie had himself carried on his litter to the women's section, where Juana Alsbury and her sister were staying with the other women and children. Gregorio Esparza's wife and children were there. Susannah Dickinson was there, with her daughter, Angelina, and Mrs. Juana Melton, the wife of Quartermaster Eliel Melton, and Concepción Losoya and her son. Sick as he was, Bowie chatted with the ladies about the coming of the Gonzales group, and other news of the day. His purpose was always to reassure them.

On March 3, Colonel Travis sat down that day to write his last message to the government—an appeal to the president in Washington-on-the-Brazos: "A blood red banner waves from the church of Bexar, and in the camp above us, in token that the war is one of vengeance against rebels," he said, and ended his report, "*God and Texas!—Victory or Death!!*"

That same day, more good news arrived for Santa Anna from General Urrea: After defeating Col. Frank W. Johnson at San Patricio, he had caught Dr. Grant at Agua Dulce Creek, returning from an expedition to find horses along the Rio Grande. The Mexicans had laid an ambush, and by the time the firing ended all the rebels were dead.

Urrea said he was now preparing to deal with Fannin, but when the general sent scouts to Goliad they reported that there was no activity at that place. The scouts were right: Fannin's attempt to reach the Alamo had failed, and he was now back at Goliad, wondering what to do.

Jim Bowie came to see Mrs. Alsbury again that night, and they talked for a while. He went back to his room. She would never see him again alive or dead.

That night, John Smith saddled up once more. He was leaving again to seek help for the beleaguered garrison of the Alamo. Colonel Travis wrote an appeal for powder and shot to Washington, and personal letters to his friend Jesse Grimes and to David Ayers, who was boarding Travis's son: "Take care of

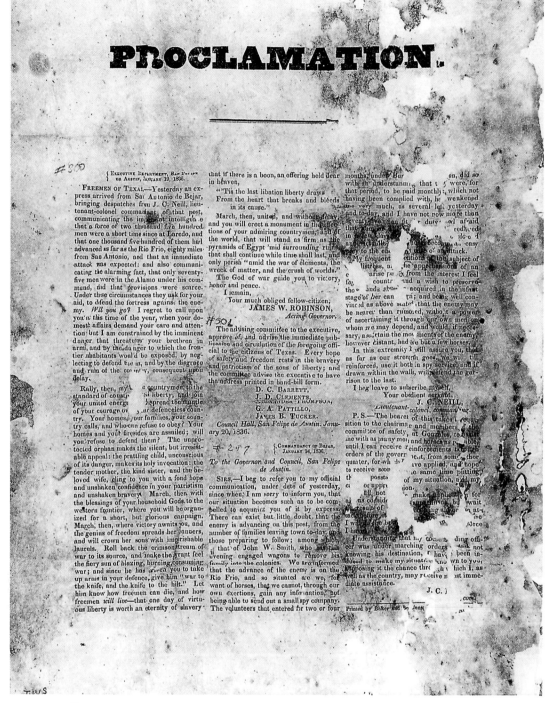

PROCLAMATION.

Executive Department, San Felipe de Austin, January 19, 1836.

FREEMEN OF TEXAS.—Yesterday an express arrived from San Antonio de Bejar, bringing despatches from J. C. Neill, lieutenant-colonel commandant of that post, communicating the important intelligence that a force of two thousand five hundred men were a short time since at Laredo, and that one thousand five hundred of them had advanced as far as the Rio Frio, eighty miles from San Antonio, and that an immediate attack was expected: and also communicating the alarming fact, that only seventy-five men were in the Alamo under his command, and that provisions were scarce. Under these circumstances they ask for your aid, to defend the fortress against the enemy. Will you go? I regret to call upon you at this time of the year, when your domestic affairs demand your care and attention: but I am constrained by the imminent danger that threatens your brethren in arms, and by the danger to which the frontier inhabitants would be exposed, by neglecting to defend them, and by the disgrace and ruin of the country, consequent upon delay.

Rally, then, my countrymen, to the standard of constitutional liberty, and join your united energy, spread the mantle of your courage over your defenceless country. Your homes, your families, your country calls, and who can refuse to obey? Your homes and your firesides are assailed; will you refuse to defend them? The unprotected orphan makes the silent, but irresistible appeal: the prattling child, unconscious of its danger, makes its holy invocation: the tender mother, the kind sister, and the beloved wife, cling to you with a fond hope and unshaken confidence in your patriotism and unshaken bravery. March, then, with the blessings of your household Gods, to the western frontier, where you will be organized for a short, but glorious campaign. March, then, where victory awaits you, and the genius of freedom spreads her banners, and will crown her sons with imperishable laurels. Roll back the crimson stream of war to its source, and make the tyrant feel the fiery sun of blazing, burning, consuming war; and since he has forced you to take up arms in your defence, give him "war to the knife, and the knife to the hilt." Let him know how freemen can die, and how freemen will live—that one day of virtuous liberty is worth an eternity of slavery

that if there is a boon, an offering held dear in heaven,

"'Tis the last libation liberty draws
From the heart that breaks and bleeds in its cause."

March, then, united, and without delay, and you will erect a monument in the affections of your admiring countrymen, and of the world, that will stand as firm as the pyramids of Egypt 'mid surrounding ruins that shall continue while time shall last, and only perish "amid the war of elements, the wreck of matter, and the crush of worlds." The God of war guide you to victory, honor and peace.

I remain,

Your much obliged fellow-citizen,

JAMES W. ROBINSON,

Acting Governor.

The advising committee to the executive, approve of, and advise the immediate publication and circulation of the foregoing official to the citizens of Texas. Every hope of safety and freedom rests in the bravery and patriotism of the sons of liberty; and the committee advise the executive to have the address printed in hand-bill form.

D. C. BARRETT,
J. D. CLEMENTS,
ALEXANDER THOMPSON,
G. A. PATTILLO,
JAMES B. TUCKER.

Council Hall, San Felipe de Austin. January 20, 1836.

Commandancy of Bejar, January 14, 1836.

To the Governor and Council, San Felipe de Austin.

SIRS,—I beg to refer you to my official communication, under date of yesterday, since when, I am sorry to inform you, that our situation becomes such as to be compelled to acquaint you of it by express. There can exist but little doubt, that the enemy is advancing on this post, from the number of families leaving town to-day, and those preparing to follow; among which, that of John W. Smith, who has this evening engaged wagons to remove his family into the colonies. We are informed that the advance of the enemy is on the Rio Frio, and so situated are we, for want of horses, that we cannot, through our own exertions, gain any information, not being able to send out a small spy company. The volunteers that entered for two or four

months under Bur...on, did so with an understanding, that t...s were, for that period, to be paid monthly; which not having been complied with, he weakened...me very much, as several left yesterday, and to-day, and I have not now more than seventy five men fit for duty...and af-aid that...families...reduced in...few days...liked...that...families...become...easy prey to the en...at any...of...attack. My frequent...citions on the subject of distress, a...he apprehensions of an...e...arise p...y from the interest I feel for...country...and a wish to preserve...tho...ands...acquired in the infant stage of her can...gn; and being well convinced as above stat...that the enemy may be nearer than rumored, without a power of ascertaining it through our own men, on whom we may depend, and would, if necessary, ascertain the movements of the enemy, however distant, had we but a few horses.

In this extremity I will assure you, that, as far as our strength goes, we will, till reinforced, use it both in spy service, and if drawn within the walls, will defend the garrison to the last.

I beg leave to subscribe myself,

Your obedient servant,

J. C. NEILL,

Lieutenant-colonel, commanding.

P.S.—The bearer of this takes requisition to the chairman and members of the committee of safety, at Gonzales, to assist me with as many men and horses as possible, until I can receive reinforcements through orders of the govern...ent, from som...thor quarter, for wh...h...ve applied, and hope to receive soon...e same time putting th...posses...of my situation, and my...or appr...ion...all not...make applicati...n for...as consid...wait...result of...ng a...r n a...ufacture it...I wil...be...force I have...

Understanding that...was under marching orders not knowing his destination, I hav...been induced to make my situati...nown to you, supposing it the chance thr...gh...hich I, as well as the country, may receive...st immediate assistance.

J. C. ...

Printed by Baker and Bor...Jons...

COL. FRANK W. JOHNSON POSES WITH A FAMOUS PORTRAIT OF STEPHEN F. AUSTIN. FROM *TEXIAN ANNUAL*, 1886.
TEXAS STATE LIBRARY & ARCHIVES COMMISSION

my little boy. If the country should be saved, I may make for him a splendid fortune; but if the country be lost and I should perish, he will have nothing but the proud recollection that he is the son of a man who died for his country."

He walked to the plaza and handed the packet of letters to John Smith. Then he had an afterthought, and quickly wrote: "Tell the reinforcements to bring ten days' rations with them." The Alamo gate swung open. A party of Texians slipped out, worked their way toward the sugar mill, and began firing. The Mexican artillery answered, and a Mexican patrol rushed to the scene of the commotion. Under cover of the activity, John Smith slipped through the gate, turned eastward, and vanished in the darkness.

TEXAS
FOREVER!!

The usurper of the South has failed in his efforts to enslave the freemen of Texas.

The wives and daughters of Texas will be saved from the brutality of Mexican soldiers.

Now is the time to emigrate to the Garden of America.

A free passage, and all found, is offered at New Orleans to all applicants. Every settler receives a location of

EIGHT HUNDRED ACRES OF LAND.

On the 23d of February, a force of 1000 Mexicans came in sight of San Antonio, and on the 25th Gen. St. Anna arrived at that place with 2500 more men, and demanded a surrender of the fort held by 150 Texians, and on the refusal, he attempted to storm the fort, twice, with his whole force, but was repelled with the loss of 500 men, and the Americans lost none. Many of his troops, the liberals of Zacatecas, are brought on to Texas in irons and are urged forward with the promise of the women and plunder of Texas.

The Texian forces were marching to relieve St. Antonio, March the 2d. The Government of Texas is supplied with plenty of arms, ammunition, provisions, &c. &c.

THIS BROADSIDE, ADVERTISING LAND IN TEXAS, GIVES A HIGHLY EXAGGERATED AND INACCURATE ACCOUNT OF THE SUCCESS OF THE ALAMO GARRISON'S DEFENSE BEFORE MARCH 6:

"ON THE 23RD OF FEBRUARY, A FORCE OF 1000 MEXICANS CAME IN SIGHT OF SAN ANTONIO, AND ON THE 25TH GENERAL SANTA ANNA ARRIVED AT THAT PLACE WITH 2500 MORE MEN AND DEMANDED A SURRENDER OF THE FORT HELD BY 150 TEXIANS, AND ON THE REFUSAL HE ATTEMPTED TO STORM THE FORT, TWICE, BUT WAS REPELLED WITH THE LOSS OF 500 MEN AND THE AMERICANS LOST NONE. MANY OF HIS TROOPS, THE LIBERALS OF ZACATECAS, ARE BROUGHT ON TO TEXAS IN IRONS AND ARE URGED FORWARD WITH THE PROMISE OF THE WOMEN AND PLUNDER OF TEXAS.

THE TEXIAN FORCES WERE MARCHING TO RELIEVE SAN ANTONIO ON MARCH 2ND. THE GOVERNMENT OF TEXAS IS SUPPLIED WITH PLENTY OF ARMS, AMMUNITION, PROVISIONS &C&C."

CENTER FOR AMERICAN HISTORY, UNIVERSITY OF TEXAS AT AUSTIN

More than any other single event in the Texas War for Independence, the Battle of the Alamo inspired Texians to win their freedom from Mexico. *Dawn at the Alamo*, an oil painting by Henry A. McArdle from 1905, is a grand-scale depiction of the famous battle. It portrays many of the battle's main characters: Col. William Travis, James Bowie, Davy Crockett, Susannah Dickinson, and Mexican commanders General Castrillón and Colonel Almonte. At one time the painting was displayed in the Texas State Capitol Senate Chambers, but it was destroyed and repainted in 1905.
Texas State Library & Archives Commission

Before Texas sought independence from Mexico, *empresarios* like Stephen F. Austin settled families in the lands controlled by Spain, then by Mexico. Austin drew this map of Texas with parts of adjoining states in 1833, and it is acknowledged as one of the first finely-detailed and accurate maps of Texas published. It covers most of Texas and parts of the Mexican states of Tamaulipas, Nuevo Leon, and Coahuila; it shows rivers, Austin's and DeWitt's colonies, towns, missions, routes and trails—including the Old San Antonio Road, silver mines, Indian tribes and villages, and herds of wild horses and game.
Texas State Library & Archives Commission

STEPHEN F. AUSTIN, "THE FATHER OF TEXAS," SETTLED 300 FAMILIES IN 1822 IN THE COLONY ESTABLISHED BY HIS FATHER, MOSES AUSTIN. EVENTUALLY, AUSTIN SETTLED MORE THAN 1,000 FAMILIES IN THE LAND HE WOULD HELP TO MAKE AN INDEPENDENT REPUBLIC. THIS PAINTING, TITLED *SETTLEMENT OF AUSTIN'S COLONY* OR *THE LOG CABIN*, WAS PAINTED BY HENRY A. MCARDLE IN OIL IN 1875. IT NOW HANGS IN THE TEXAS STATE CAPITOL IN AUSTIN.
TEXAS STATE LIBRARY & ARCHIVES COMMISSION

COL. WILLIAM BARRET TRAVIS COMMANDED THE FORCE AT THE ALAMO THAT FACED SANTA ANNA'S ARMY. THIS PAINTING BY LOUIS EYTH, *THE SPEECH OF TRAVIS TO HIS MEN AT THE ALAMO* (CIRCA 1878), SEEMS TO HAVE BEEN LOST. THIS PHOTOGRAPH IS FROM PAULINE PINCKNEY'S BOOK *PAINTING IN TEXAS*.
DAUGHTERS OF THE REPUBLIC OF TEXAS LIBRARY

JAMES BOWIE SHARED COMMAND OF THE
ALAMO GARRISON WITH COLONEL TRAVIS
UNTIL ILLNESS FORCED HIM TO TAKE TO
HIS BED. THIS PAINTING OF BOWIE IS
ARTIST MAMIE CARDWELL'S 1894 COPY OF
AN EARLIER WORK BY GEORGE P. A.
HEALY.
*TEXAS STATE LIBRARY & ARCHIVES
COMMISSION*

THE MOST FAMOUS OF THE ALAMO DEFENDERS WAS DAVID
CROCKETT, A FRONTIERSMAN AND FORMER MEMBER OF
CONGRESS. HE ARRIVED IN SAN ANTONIO DE BÉXAR WITH
THE TENNESSEE MOUNTED VOLUNTEERS ABOUT TWO WEEKS
BEFORE THE MEXICAN ARMY SURROUNDED THE ALAMO. THIS
PORTRAIT BY WILLIAM HENRY HUDDLE HANGS IN THE SOUTH
FOYER OF THE TEXAS STATE CAPITOL IN AUSTIN.
TEXAS STATE LIBRARY & ARCHIVES COMMISSION

THE FIRST MEXICAN GUNS FIRED ON THE ALAMO IN THE EARLY AFTERNOON OF FEBRUARY 24, 1836, BUT THE FINAL ASSAULT BEGAN IN EARNEST ON MARCH 6. THIS PAINTING SHOWING THE BEGINNING OF THE ASSAULT, *FALL OF THE ALAMO*, WAS PAINTED BY THEODORE GENTILZ IN 1885.
TEXAS STATE LIBRARY & ARCHIVES COMMISSION

FOR NINETY MINUTES, THE DESPERATE STRUGGLE RAGED AS THE ALAMO'S WALLS WERE BREACHED AND THE DEFENDERS TOOK ON THE MEXICAN FORCES IN HAND-TO-HAND FIGHTING. *THE SIEGE OF THE ALAMO* WAS PAINTED BY L. R. BROMLEY OF CHICAGO IN 1884. THE PARAPET ON THE CHAPEL WAS NOT THERE AT THE TIME OF THE BATTLE BUT WAS ADDED TO THE CHAPEL IN 1849 BY THE U.S. ARMY.
TEXAS STATE LIBRARY & ARCHIVES COMMISSION

During his term as a member of Congress, David Crockett sat for this James H. Shegogue watercolor portrait. It was painted in 1831, five years before Crockett's death at the Alamo.
National Portrait Gallery, Smithsonian Institution

A battle scene of the fighting in the barracks rooms of the Alamo shows the hand-to-hand combat of the defenders' final struggles. This photoengraving, *The Last Stand in the Alamo*, appeared in *Texas History Stories* by E. D. Littlejohn in 1901. *Texas State Library & Archives Commission*

FOLLOWING THE FALL OF THE ALAMO AND THE GOLIAD MASSACRE, THE TEXAS ARMY FOUGHT ITS FINAL BATTLE FOR FREEDOM AT SAN JACINTO. FORTIFIED BY A DESIRE TO AVENGE THEIR FALLEN COMRADES, THE TEXIANS AND TEJANOS ROUTED THE ENEMY AND CAPTURED GENERAL SANTA ANNA. *THE BATTLE OF SAN JACINTO*, AN OIL PAINTING BY I. M. D. GUILLAUME, WAS PAINTED IN 1892.
COURTESY OF THE R. W. NORTON ART GALLERY, SHREVEPORT, LOUISIANA

AT SAN JACINTO, THE TEXAS ARMY FOUGHT BENEATH THIS BATTLE FLAG. "LIBERTY OR DEATH" READS THE BANNER DRAPED OVER THE SWORD HELD ALOFT BY THE LADY LIBERTY. THE FLAG NOW HANGS IN THE CHAMBER OF THE TEXAS HOUSE OF REPRESENTATIVES IN AUSTIN. THIS REVERSE VIEW WAS REDISCOVERED DURING CONSERVATION EFFORTS.
TEXAS STATE LIBRARY & ARCHIVES COMMISSION

THE OUTRAGE FELT BY THE TEXAS ARMY AFTER THE ALAMO AND GOLIAD BROUGHT A NEW FEROCITY TO ITS FIGHTING. FOR MANY OF THE TEXIANS AND TEJANOS ON THE BATTLEFIELD, SAN JACINTO PROVIDED A WAY TO AVENGE FRIENDS, RELATIVES, AND COMRADES-IN-ARMS. THIS 1895 OIL PAINTING BY HENRY A. MCARDLE, *THE BATTLE OF SAN JACINTO*, NOW HANGS IN THE TEXAS STATE CAPITOL IN AUSTIN. *TEXAS STATE LIBRARY & ARCHIVES COMMISSION*

GENERAL SANTA ANNA FLED THE SAN JACINTO BATTLEFIELD, BUT WAS CAPTURED AND BROUGHT TO SURRENDER TO GENERAL HOUSTON, WHO SAT BENEATH A TREE DUE TO HIS WOUNDED FOOT. *THE SURRENDER OF SANTA ANNA* BY WILLIAM HENRY HUDDLE, PAINTED IN 1886, HANGS IN THE TEXAS STATE CAPITOL IN AUSTIN. *TEXAS STATE LIBRARY & ARCHIVES COMMISSION*

THESE BATTLE FLAGS FROM THE GUERRERO, TOLUCA, AND MATAMOROS BATTALIONS WERE CAPTURED BY TEXIANS AT THE BATTLE OF SAN JACINTO.
TEXAS STATE LIBRARY & ARCHIVES COMMISSION

FOLLOWING THE BATTLE OF SAN JACINTO THE PROVISIONAL GOVERNMENT OF TEXAS ESTABLISHED THE REPUBLIC OF TEXAS, AND SAM HOUSTON BECAME ITS FIRST PRESIDENT. THIS $50 BILL FROM CURRENCY ISSUED BY THE REPUBLIC IN 1840 BEARS A SMALL IMAGE OF STEPHEN F. AUSTIN ON THE RIGHT.
TEXAS STATE LIBRARY & ARCHIVES COMMISSION

FOLLOWING THE FAMOUS BATTLE AT THE ALAMO, THE OLD MISSION STOOD IN RUINS FOR MANY YEARS. THIS PAINTING BY THEODORE GENTILZ SHOWS THE RUINS FROM THE PERIOD OF THE 1840S, BEFORE ITS RESTORATION. TODAY, THE ALAMO IS MAINTAINED BY THE DAUGHTERS OF THE REPUBLIC OF TEXAS.
THE DAUGHTERS OF THE REPUBLIC OF TEXAS LIBRARY

William Barret Travis
1809=1836

As a lieutenant colonel in the regular Texas Army, William Barret Travis was the acting commander of the Alamo when it was attacked by General Santa Anna's forces. Before that, he had been a prominent member of the Texas War Party, which advocated rebellion against Mexico before it was popular.

Travis was born in South Carolina but educated in Alabama, where he worked as a teacher, newspaper editor, and lawyer. He had come to Texas in 1831 from Alabama, abandoning his pregnant wife and child. In Texas, he established a law partnership in Nacogdoches with Patrick Jack, another recent arrival. Soon Travis was known as a ladies' man as well as a lawyer, although most of his conquests were prostitutes or slaves.

In the Anahuac Incident on Galveston Bay, he became involved in the questions of civil rights and abuses of authority. He was a brave, sometimes precipitate man with a yearning for glory that was common to many of the young immigrants to Texas. When General Santa Anna appeared at San Antonio with his demand for unconditional surrender, Travis knew that his moment of glory had arrived. His response was a shot fired from the largest cannon in the fort. After that he let it be known that the terms were victory or death, and that anyone who wished to leave was free to go. All those assembled in the Alamo save one elected to stand with Travis, and they died heroic deaths on the morning of March 6, 1836.

A PAINTING OF COL. WILLIAM BARRET TRAVIS, THE COMMANDER OF THE ALAMO. *TEXAS STATE LIBRARY & ARCHIVES COMMISSION*

It was obvious that the Mexicans were going to attack the north side of the Alamo. The defenders threw up more dirt to cushion the wall against cannon balls, creating a hill ten feet high that sloped down toward the Alamo plaza. A man could reach the top of the wall simply by climbing the slope. But the obverse to this was that if the Mexicans could get to the top of the wall, they could march down into the Alamo. And now there was no shelter for riflemen at the north wall. Yes, that was the weak point, and from the way Santa Anna had sited his cannon, it was apparent that the Mexicans knew it.

True to promise, the Alamo's eighteen-pounder fired three times a day, and people as far away as Gonzales could hear it.

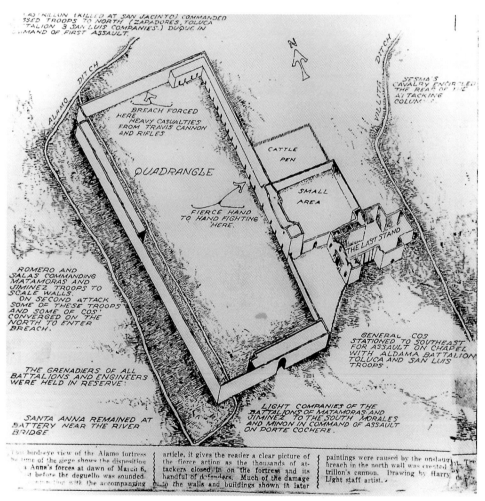

DIAGRAM OF THE MEXICAN ATTACK ON THE ALAMO, MARCH 6, 1836, SHOWING THE DISPOSITION OF MEXICAN TROOPS AND INDICATING THE AREAS OF FIGHTING. FROM A DRAWING BY A MEMBER OF THE STAFF OF THE *SAN ANTONIO LIGHT*. *TEXAS STATE LIBRARY & ARCHIVES COMMISSION*

TO THE PEOPLE OF TEXAS.

COUNCIL HALL, SAN FELIPE DE AUSTIN
FEB. 13th 1836.

War with its most terrific attendants and consequences is rolling its horrors upon us! The enemy with great force is within our borders;—and Texas sleeping amidst surrounding dangers. The arch enemy of Liberty—Santa Anna, prompted by vindictive fury, leads the onset,—death, violation and extermination are determined against us. The following letters speak a language not to be misunderstood and clearly show, the alarming situation of the country and the necessity for prompt and efficient action. If we would save our country from the threatened destruction, our wives and daughters from the vilest pollution, and our families and ourselves from general massacre, FREEMEN OF TEXAS—*now is the hour!!* —let no consideration prevent you from coming *boldly forth* TO THE RESCUE!—Our brethren from the United States are, by hundreds in the field, leading the van guard for our defence; and shall we look to others alone, for that protection from dangers so alarming? NO TEXIANS! *shoulder your Rifles,* join our PATRIOTIC FRIENDS, and by one united and well directed effort, teach the *Tyrant of Mexico* and his hirelings that *the sons of the* BRAVE PATRIOTS OF '76 *are invincible in the cause of* FREEDOM *and the* RIGHTS OF MAN.

D. C. BARRETT,—*Chr'n.*
J. D. CLEMENTS,
ALEX. THOMPSON,
G. A. PATTILLO,
JOHN McMULLEN,
JOHN MALONE,
JOHN S. LANE.

SAN PATRICIO, FEB. 6th 1836.

Dear Sir!

Don Placido Benavides has just arrived, & brings disagreeable intelligence. Gonzales' command is entirely dispersed, and twenty two men taken prisoners. Three hundred Cavalry and three hundred Infantry have arrived at Matamoras, which in addition to the Garrison makes the effective force now there 1000 men, and more are expected shortly. Cos and *all* his officers from Bejar are raising troops to march on Texas. One thousand men are already on the Rio Frio. One thousand more on the march near the Rio Grande destined for some point of Texas; and forces are gathering rapidly in all directions for the same object. It is believed that an attack is intended on Goliad and Bejar simultaneously.

Roderigus has broken his parole since 5 o'clock this evening and as I have but 18 effective men here and no horses, I could not pursue him.

The inhabitants of Tamaulipas are generally in favor of (1824,) but are so much oppressed by the military, that many of the principal men having been arrested they are completely fettered. Santa Anna caused a report to be set afloat that he was with the troops at Matamoras, but it is ascertained beyond all doubt that he is on the way to the Rio Grande for the purpose of pushing on those forces.

Don Placido deems it of the utmost importance that troops be sent to Bejar as well as others retained in this direction and also assures me that Santa Anna wishes to draw the troops of Texas out to Matamoras in hopes to throw a strong force in their rear while he makes his attack on the upper part of the Colonies. This information he received from the first alcalde of Matamoras. He has been within 20 leagues of the town and corresponded with him.

The people of Tamaulipas as well as those of the Rio Grande complain much of Dimitt's Proclamation, and would have acted with more decision were it not for that act, but they fear it is now almost impossible; but are still anxious for the cause. The Cavalry are the choice troops from the interior, they are armed, every one, with lance musket, pistols and sword and Santa Anna has sworn to TAKE TEXAS OR LOSE MEXICO.

Doct. Grant has been out two days with thirty men. I feel very anxious about him. I intended to have sent you more wagons to-morrow morning early, and in fact had the oxen yoked to start before day-light but shall now await your further orders.

Cos is actually with Seizma and also U-gartchiers. They have 1000 spare horses and a large number of pack mules.

It is with regret, but I am absolutely obliged to give Doct. Hoit your horse to carry him with this.

Yours most sincerely,
ROBERT MORRIS.

P. S. To raise funds and provisions, Cos causes each man to give an inventory of all he possesses with valuation of each article on which he demands one per cent, every twenty days, he then sends two men to make the appraisement over, and if he finds that they make a return higher than the owners, he demands three per cent in lieu of one; and each family has to furnish a fanega of corn also, every twenty days, and even causes the women to grind it, without respect to station. His soldiers have assassinated many of the most influential citizens, and the wives and daughters are prostituted—the whole country is given up to the troops to induce them forward. R. M.

MISSION OF REFUJIO, 10 o'clok P. M.
7th Feb. 1836.

To his Excellency,
J. W. ROBINSON—Gov. &c. AND GENERAL COUNCIL.

I have to communicate to you, & through you to the people of Texas, the inclosed express just received from the advance Division of the volunteer army:—

You will readily discover the great difference between this information, and that contained in my report of the 3rd inst. The first was then supposed to be entitled to credit, and accordingly made the subject of a communication;—I cannot now question the correctness of the last,—Not the least doubt should any longer be entertained, by any friend of Texas, of the design of Santa Anna to overrun the country, and expel or exterminate, every white man within its borders;—May I be permitted to ask of them in sober earnestness, "Why halt ye, between two opinions? Your soil is again to be polluted by the foot steps of the hirelings of an unprincipled Despot!! Will the freemen of Texas calmly fold their arms and await, until the approach of their deadly enemy, compels them to protect their own fire sides? Can it be possible that they—that any American can so far forget the Honor of their Mothers, wives and daughters, as not to fly to their Rifles, and march to meet the Tyrant, and avenge the insults and wrongs inflicted on his own country-women, on Rio Grande? What can be expected for the *fair Daughters* of chaste *white women,* when their own country women are prostituted by a licensed soldiery, as an inducement to push forward into the Colonies, where they may find *fairer game?*

The question, would seem, to be useless; but when I tell you, that among the rise of 400 men at, and near this post, I doubt if twenty-five citizens of Texas can be mustered in the ranks—nay, I am informed, whilst writing the above, that there is not half that number;—Does not this fact, bespeake an indifference, and criminal apathy, truly alarming? We calculate upon the service of our volunteer friends, to aid in the defence and protection of our soil—Do the citizens of Texas reflect for a moment, that these men, many of whom, have served since November last, have not received the first *cents wages,* and are now; nearly naked; and many of them bare-footed, or what is tantamount to it; could they hear the just complaints and taunting remarks in regard to the *absence of the* old settlers and owners of the soil, and total neglect in the officers of the Government; not providing them with even the necessaries of life, this our main stay would not be so confidently relied on!! Will you allow me to recommend the issuing of *general orders,* to be sent by expresses to every part of Texas, commanding the civic militia, under their present organization, to turn out & march forthwith to the seat of war. At the same time call upon all volunteers to do the same, taking care, to apprise our friends in the U. S. of our true situation, that a sufficient inducement may be held out to draw them to our standard, in this hour of trial—It is generally believed in the United States, that the war, is over, and indeed our own citizens seem to have indulged the same hope,—We are now undeceived, and unless, a turn out *in mass* be made, and that speedily, the force now in the field cannot keep the invaders in check, long enough to prevent the fury of the war's being waged in the heart of the country, if ever Santa Anna crosses the Guadaloupe with 5,000 men, we have to fight east of the Brazos, if not the Trinity! I feel certain that, even in that event, his army would inevitably perish or surrender. But, should we not prevent such a dreadful catastrophe, and rally to the rescue, every freeman of Texas!! Evince your determination to live free or perish in the ditch.

In order to provide for the wants of the men, appoint contractors, and have established on the different routes west, depots, for beef, cattle, salt &c., and such provisions as may be obtained, that the men may be pushed forward without delay, to such points as may be deemed most exposed. In the mean time, I would respectfully recommend such measures be taken, as to form a corps of reserve on Colorado, at or between Bastrop and Gonzales, and also the Navidad & La Baca, in order to protect the settlers, and cover the advance, in case an enemy with a superior force, should leave them in their rear, and march forward, calculating much upon our weakness and unprepared state of defence, and expecting much from our inexperience and division of forces, which might be dispersed in detail, & leave the country an easy prey, to the arch Tyrant.

It is useless to contravert the fact that our

NOTICE AND REPORT FROM SAN FELIPE OF EVENTS IN SAN ANTONIO IN EARLY FEBRUARY 1836 "TO THE PEOPLE OF TEXAS."
TEXAS STATE LIBRARY & ARCHIVES COMMISSION

At dawn on March 4, the Mexicans began firing the Gaona cannon, but the Alamo returned few shots; the fort was short of powder and cannon balls.

Colonel Travis surveyed his domain: everything had been done that could to shore up the defenses. Weak points in the wall had been strengthened, parapets had been erected to cover the riflemen, and earthworks built to cover the main gate. Davy Crockett's Tennesseeans had volunteered to hold the weak point of the palisade that ran from the church to the wall on the south side. A break in the north wall had been shored up with timbers and earth. But the fact remained, as Colonel Travis knew all too well, that this was not a fort but a Spanish mission, and its walls were not built for defense against artillery.

The Mexicans were on all sides now: in San Antonio, 400 yards west; in La Villita, 300 yards south; at the powderhouse, 1,000 yards southeast; on the ditch, 800 yards northeast; and at the mill, 800 yards north. It was hard not to be discouraged. As Davy Crockett put it: "I think we ought to march out and die in the open air. I don't like to be hemmed up."

The slowdown in action had been evident for several days. Santa Anna was still waiting for his twelve-pound cannon, but on the afternoon of March 4, a sudden quiet descended on San Antonio. It was eerie. What the defenders did not know was that Santa Anna had called a conference of senior officers, a very unusual step for this self-willed general. He wanted to know whether or not the time had come to assault the Alamo.

General Sesma said yes.

Colonel Almonte said yes.

General Cós said no.

Everyone had his say, but no general agreement was reached. Santa Anna lost his temper. Then he dismissed the meeting, saying he would decide the next day.

After the meeting, Santa Anna sat down to consider his options. The twelve-pounders would be useful—no denying that. But if they waited, he had indications that the Alamo might be reinforced. Fannin had 350 men at Goliad, and Santa Anna's spies told him that they were ready to march. Three or four hundred more in the face of four thousand might not seem much, but that meant more delay in rooting out this rebellion.

By two o'clock on the afternoon of March 5 the decision was made. "We will attack tomorrow morning," Santa Anna told Colonel Almonte.

The Unanimous
Declaration of Independence
made by the
Delegates of the People of Texas
in General Convention
at the Town of Washington
on the 2nd day of March 1836

When a Government has ceased
to protect the lives liberty and property
of the people, from whom its legitimate
powers are derived, and for the advance-
ment of whose happiness it was insti-
tuted; and so far from being a guarantee for the enjoyment of those inesti-
mable and inalienable rights becomes
an instrument in the hands of evil
rulers for their oppression: When the
Federal Republican Constitution
of their Country, which they have sworn
to support, no longer has a substantial existence, and the whole nature of
their government has been forcibly changed, without their consent, from a
restricted federative republic, composed
of sovereign states, to a Consolidated

FIRST PAGE OF THE TWELVE-PAGE HANDWRITTEN DECLARATION OF
INDEPENDENCE OF TEXAS, MARCH 2, 1836.
TEXAS STATE LIBRARY & ARCHIVES COMMISSION

The End of the Matamoros Expedition

Frank Johnson and Dr. James Grant had fought bravely in the Battle of San Antonio, and Dr. Grant had been wounded there. Now, in the late winter of 1836, they wanted to be off on their expedition to the rich city of Matamoros. Time and Sam Houston's negative arguments had already caused considerable attrition in their force. With the backing of the Interim Council they had stripped the San Antonio and Goliad garrisons of supplies, but by mid-February their group of volunteers had dwindled to ninety men, including about fifty of the New Orleans Greys. They moved to San Patricio. Here they separated. Dr. Grant went off with half the men to the south, to round up some wild mustangs. Frank Johnson stayed on at San Patricio with thirty-four men to guard the horse herds. He had separated his men into five groups, two of which protected the horse herds while the others were off duty.

Meanwhile, General Urrea had crossed the Rio Grande and begun his sweep through the coastal prairie. At three o'clock on the morning of February 27, in a driving rainstorm, Urrea surprised the Johnson group at San Patricio. The attack came with such surprise and ferocity that Johnson had no chance to rally his men, and by daybreak ten Texians were killed and eighteen taken prisoner. Only Johnson and six of his men escaped into the countryside.

Questioning the prisoners, General Urrea learned Dr. Grant's plans and the route he would follow to bring his wild horses to San Patricio. He set up an ambush at Agua Dulce Creek, twenty miles south of San Patricio.

On March 2, Dr. Grant and his men sprang the trap. Grant, Placido Benavides, and Reuben Brown were out front, while the main body of men brought up the 300 head of horses they had captured. As the main body passed through a draw, sixty Mexican lancers swooped down on them. Grant looked back and saw that his command had been cut off. He instructed Benavides to ride on to Goliad, to warn Colonel Fannin that Urrea was in the area and on the hunt.

Benavides rode off while Dr. Grant and Brown went back to join their comrades. As they drew near, they could see that most of the party were already dead. A Mexican lancer stabbed Brown's horse, but Brown grabbed another one and rode on. At that moment the herd stampeded, breaking its way through the Mexican cavalry, and Dr. Grant and Brown joined the wild mustangs in their flight. The Mexicans pursued. A dragoon charged Brown, who shot him as he raised his lance. Other Mexican cavalrymen came up and called on the two men to surrender. But the two Texians continued to fly.

They had galloped about seven miles when they were surrounded. They dismounted and prepared to fight. A Mexican lancer stabbed Brown in the arm, but Dr. Grant shot the lancer out of the saddle. Then Grant was pierced by several lances, and Brown was lassoed and dragged along the ground. At Urrea's headquarters, Brown was questioned and then sent to Matamoros for more questioning. Before he went, he saw several officers run their swords into Dr. Grant's corpse. He learned that Grant had a reputation in Mexico as an ungrateful opportunist. One version of the story has it that when the lancers learned Grant was a doctor, they offered him a passport if he would treat their wounded. After Grant treated the wounded, he asked for the passport. His hands were tied to the tail of a wild mustang and his feet to the legs. The mustang was then set free and kicked the doctor to death.

That was the last gasp of the ill-fated Matamoros Expedition.

TEN

❧

The Fall of the Alamo

At five o'clock on the afternoon of March 5, the Mexican grenadiers moved quietly out of San Antonio to join the Zapadores in the assembly area. There was a lull in the Mexican artillery fire, and some of the defenders of the Alamo saw troops moving around. As the firing stopped, the defenders emerged from shelter and began cooking their dinners over open fires in front of the chapel. Mrs. Dickinson persuaded James Bonham to have a cup of tea.

Suddenly Colonel Travis called an assembly. The tired men grumbled a bit, but they roused themselves and assembled in the open plaza. Mrs. Dickinson hovered in the rear as Travis addressed the men.

He declared that there was no longer any real hope of substantial reinforcement. But there were still choices: They could surrender, take their chances on escape over the wall, or stay and fight to the end, which might delay the Mexican advance into Texas. As for himself, he was determined to stay and fight. He urged the garrison to join him, but he left the decision to each man to make for himself.

Louis Rose
1786-1850

They called Louis Rose "the coward of the Alamo," but in fact he was an experienced mercenary soldier of Napoleon's army who had remained in Mexico. The mystery was, what was he doing at the Alamo at all?

He listened to Colonel Travis's valedictory speech the night before the attack and decided that he would not throw his life away for someone else's cause. Until this point he had stood by the cannon, as Enrique Esparza, then a boy, recalled in later years. Rose consulted Jim Bowie and Davy Crockett, both of whom agreed that he had no real stake in the revolution; then he gathered a few belongings and went over the wall.

He slipped through the Mexican lines, avoiding Mexican settlements as he headed north. Stumbling through prickly pear and yucca country, Rose was badly scratched and nearly starved before arriving at an American settlement, where an acquaintance recognized him and took him in. In later years he told his story several times, with variations. Sometimes he told of going over the wall and landing in a pool of blood, but that was most unlikely; there was no blood at the Alamo before the final Mexican assault.

After the war, Rose went into business in eastern Texas, but he did not do well. The stigma of being the sole survivor of the defense force stuck to him. Ultimately he moved to Louisiana, where he died in 1850.

One version has it that Travis drew a line in the sand with his sword and crossed it, then asked all those who would stay to join him. Susannah Dickinson did not mention a line; she said that he asked any man who wanted to leave to step out of line. One man, Louis Rose, a grizzled French veteran of Napoleon's army, stepped out. All the others elected to stay, including Jim Bowie, who was so sick he had to be brought on a pallet to the assembly. Then the men went back to their fires and their dinners. Louis Rose consulted with Jim Bowie and Davy Crockett. They both wished him Godspeed, although Bowie thought he would not succeed in escaping through the lines. Rose picked up his slender bag of belongings, slipped over the wall in the gathering darkness, and was gone.

COL. WILLIAM BARRET TRAVIS GAVE THE MEN UNDER HIS COMMAND THE OPTION
TO SURRENDER OR LEAVE THE ALAMO BEFORE THE FINAL ASSAULT BEGAN.
POPULAR LEGEND CLAIMS THAT TRAVIS DREW A LINE IN THE SAND WITH HIS
SWORD AND ASKED THAT THOSE WILLING TO STAY AND FIGHT TO CROSS IT. *THE
SPEECH OF TRAVIS TO HIS MEN AT THE ALAMO* (CIRCA 1878), IS BASED ON THIS
EVENT.
TEXAS STATE LIBRARY & ARCHIVES COMMISSION

At seven o'clock, the members of the Matamoros battalion and the members of the Jimenez battalion lay down to sleep. So did the men of the Aldama
and Toluca battalions. Darkness came early, but no matter, these were seasoned
soldiers who had learned to take their rest when they could. At eight o'clock, the
men of the San Luis battalion pulled out of the line and sought rest.

By ten o'clock, the city of San Antonio was silent.

In the Alamo, Colonel Travis was very much awake. He composed another
message to Goliad. His experienced couriers were all gone, but sixteen-year-old
Jim Allen was begging for a chance to show what he could do. Travis handed
him the dispatch, the gate opened, and young Allen dashed through on his bay
mare, riding bareback, Indian style. He galloped unharmed through the
Mexican lines.

Travis walked around the Alamo, checking the three pickets who had been
posted outside the wall to warn of surprise attack. He spent a few minutes in the
chapel, talking to the children. To little Angelina Dickinson he gave his gold ring
with a cat's-eye stone; he threaded a string through it and placed it around her

neck. He examined the defenses again—the men had been working to repair damage from the last day's shelling. All that could be done had been done.

At about midnight, Travis lay down for a few hours of rest and so then did his pickets, exhausted from night after night of wakefulness, watching and listening. One by one they drifted off in their hiding places. Here the enemy's scouts found them. A quick thrust with a knife and the pickets were put to sleep forever.

The Mexican cavalrymen were the first to arise that night. They fed and watered their horses, mounted up, and rode into the fields, where their duty would be to mop up any of the Alamo defenders who managed to escape the fortress.

Mexican officers and noncommissioned officers moved through the sleeping Mexican soldiers, waking them and getting them into line, making sure that they were wearing shoes and that the ladder men would sling their rifles or muskets over their shoulders. They might forget their weapons in the excitement of attack, or forget to make sure that their bayonets were sharp. General Santa Anna was very particular about that. In the Iturbi house, which was headquarters, Santa Anna drank a cup of coffee and went over details with Colonel Almonte. Then they went out together. Ben, an American Negro who was Almonte's personal servant, was glad to see them go. Santa Anna had been unusually peevish this night.

At 1 A.M., the units were moving into their assigned positions for the jump-off. There was no sound except for shuffling feet, and an occasional cough. But the general and the colonel reappeared at headquarters just as Ben sat down for a rest. They demanded more coffee. When Ben hesitated, Santa Anna threatened to run him through with his sword. Ben snapped to and began bustling around with cups and plates while the two officers talked. Colonel Almonte spoke of casualties which, he said, would be high. Santa Anna said it could not be helped.

At 3 A.M., the general and the colonel left headquarters again, and Ben settled down to rest. The troops were getting into position: General Cós's column stopped two hundred yards northwest of the Alamo, and the men sank shivering into the cold wet grass. The reserves crossed the river and headed north into the earthworks, and the cavalry mounted and began to move out toward their assigned positions. At 4 A.M., the silence was broken only by the breathing of the soldiers as they lay in their assigned positions and waited. Santa Anna moved to the earthworks north of the Alamo. The reserves were there with the bands of the Mexican battalions.

FALL OF THE ALAMO, PAINTED BY THEODORE GENTILZ IN 1885. IT SHOWS THE MEXICANS MASSING TO ATTACK, AND THE DEFENDERS SCATTERED AROUND THE COMPOUND. THE PAINTING WAS LATER DESTROYED BY FIRE. *TEXAS STATE LIBRARY & ARCHIVES COMMISSION*

In the Alamo, Travis slept in his room, sword and double-barreled shotgun by his side. His slave Joe lay nearby.

At 5 A.M., the first light of dawn appeared on the horizon. Santa Anna's bugler was ready and put the bugle to his lips, but he was anticipated by an irrepressible soldier.

"Viva Santa Anna!" the soldier shouted.

The bugler blew the stirring call of attack, and other buglers took up the call. The bands struck up the *Deguello*, and to this stirring music the soldiers surged forward cheering, bent on revenging the disgrace of December.

"Arriba!" cried General Cós, and his troops rose from their places 200 yards north of the Alamo and ran to attack.

On the Alamo's north wall, Officer of the Day John Baugh was just starting his rounds. He turned at the sound of the bugle. He could not see the troops coming, but he could hear them. No word had come from the pickets outside the wall, but the growing noise could only mean that the enemy was attacking.

He ran into the fort, shouting, "Colonel Travis, the Mexicans are coming!"

Travis leaped up, grabbing his homespun jacket, his sword, and his shotgun. "Come on, Joe!" he shouted as he ran outside.

The enemy was coming. Rockets exploded in the sky, sending their eerie light to mingle with the dawn. No time to worry now why the pickets had not sounded the alarm. No time to realize that the pickets had been wiped out.

"Come on!" Travis shouted. "The Mexicans are upon us and we'll give 'em hell!"

Men were running, the riflemen to their positions on the parapets, the artillerymen to their guns.

"Hurrah!" Travis yelled. "Give 'em hell!" And then, seeing some of the Tejanos, he switched to Spanish. *"No reindirse, muchachos!* Don't give up!"

But it was already obvious to any who had seen that blood-red flag flying from the San Fernando church belfry, or heard the bands playing the *Deguello*, that there could be no surrender. There would be no mercy.

The Mexicans reached the ditch, where the cannon in the fort could not

STORMING OF THE ALAMO. A HIGHLY IMAGINATIVE CONCEPT WITH THE RIDER ON THE WHITE HORSE REPRESENTING SANTA ANNA URGING HIS TROOPS FORWARD. IN FACT, SANTA ANNA WAS NOT IN THE ALAMO BUT SAFELY BEHIND SOME EARTHWORKS SOME DISTANCE AWAY. FROM AN ILLUSTRATION IN *THE PICTORIAL HISTORY OF TEXAS.*
TEXAS STATE LIBRARY & ARCHIVES COMMISSION

bear down on them. The attackers brought up their scaling ladders and put them against the wall. The first wave climbed, and as their heads appeared at the top of the wall, the Texian riflemen picked them off. Colonel Travis aimed his shotgun and let go a blast. A Mexican volley rang out and Travis fell, a bullet through his head. His shotgun fell over the wall among the Mexicans, and he rolled down the bank and sat at the bottom, dying. Realizing this, Joe ran for the barracks, dived into a small storage room, and shut the door behind him. From this time on, he only heard what was happening.

In the sacristy of the chapel, Susannah Dickinson listened too. Little Angelina sat by her mother's side, clutching nervously at her mother's apron. Susannah looked up as sixteen-year-old Galba Fuqua of Gonzales burst into the room. He was holding his bloody jaw together with both hands, unable to speak. He tried to tell Mrs. Dickinson something, but could not get the words out. He tried again. Then he turned and rushed back into the fight. Mrs. Dickinson did not see him again.

The walls of the Alamo had come alive with cannon and rifle fire. Every Texian had four or five rifles at his side and Captain Dickinson's cannoneers were proving to be fast and skillful. Santa Anna, standing behind the earthworks to the north, saw the whole fortress lit up by gunfire.

To the east and south the Mexicans were stopped by the guns of the Alamo chapel on the northeast. Two blasts of grapeshot tore through the ranks of the Aldama battalion and forty men fell like straws. From the northeast another volley and a company of Tolucas was decimated. Their commander, Colonel Duque, was down with a fractured leg, but the fighting surged on around and over him.

The fire from the fort forced the first wave, Colonel Duque and Col. José María Romero, to converge on the north wall, although Santa Anna's geometric plan called for the four units to attack against four sides of the fort. The surge drove Morales's men to the left, where they finally came up against the southwest corner.

The first wave was down, but the ranks pressed on. The scaling ladders rose again. From his vantage point on the earthworks, Santa Anna watched.

What had happened to the ladder men? There had been twenty-eight ladders, but he could see only a handful, and they were rising and falling as the bodies jammed together. Three of the four columns had ended up against the north wall. The men surged and fell, the ladders fell and rose again, and above it all the bands played the *Deguello* march.

From where Santa Anna stood, the scene looked very much like summer lightning, as the flashes from the guns of the Alamo cannon mingled with the flashes from the rockets in the sky. Santa Anna ordered Col. Agustín Amat to send in the reserves. Then he ordered Colonel Almonte and the other members of his staff to go to the fort and encourage the troops.

The troops at the north wall were close enough to be protected from the fire from the Alamo cannon, but not from the rifles and muskets of their countrymen. The confusion became so great that Santa Anna grew alarmed. The 400 Grenadiers and Zapadores charged in and were decimated like the rest. The Alamo's cannon spoke, and the officers were the first to fall. Half of them were hit in the first two volleys of shrapnel, and as the reserves ran they fired blindly, too often bringing down their comrades. General Filisola, who arrived on the scene the next day, was horrified by the effects of the "friendly fire."

FRONTIER SCOUT AND FORMER CONGRESSMAN DAVY CROCKETT WAS ONE OF THE MOST FAMOUS OF THE ALAMO'S DEFENDERS. DETAIL FROM THE PORTRAIT BY WILLIAM HENRY HUDDLE SHOWS CROCKETT AS A FRONTIERSMAN. *TEXAS STATE LIBRARY & ARCHIVES COMMISSION*

"Since they attacked in a close column," he observed, "the shots were aimed at the backs of those ahead of them. Thus it was that most of our dead and wounded were caused by this misfortune. The soldiers under the wall were raked time and again by the bullets of their friends."

The human pressure at the north wall of the Alamo was unbelievable—1,500, with perhaps 500 dead under their feet, lying in a huge crescent that fanned out from the wall. At the opposite end of the Alamo, the fourth column came up against Davy Crockett's Tennesseeans, who had chosen to defend this wall. Crockett's twelve sharpshooters bit a large chunk out of the Morales unit until the colonel led them to the southwest corner of the Alamo wall, where they sat in the shadow of the wall and changed their plan of attack.

The mob scene at the north wall had drawn many Alamo defenders away from their posts. Now Colonel Morales led his men in a determined attack on the low south wall and in a few minutes seized the eighteen-pounder. The soldiers killed the gun crew, then raced down the ramp to attack the inner defenses. On the north wall, Gen. Juan Amador snapped an order and the men swung a cannon around and began blasting doorways. After seeing that Colonel Duque and Colonel Romero were down, General Castrillón rallied the troops. They streamed over the wall through the plaza, and joined up with Morales's men. The surge was too much for Quartermaster Eliel Melton and the men with him. They fled over the wall and into the open in a desperate attempt to escape. This was just what the Dolores cavalry were waiting for. Sweeping down, they hacked at the fleeing men with lance and sabre. Some cornered Texians fought back. One Texian killed a lance corporal with a blast from his double-barreled shotgun. But the sabres and lances did their grisly work and only two of the escapees managed to save themselves temporarily. One hid under a bush, only to be routed out and stabbed to death. Another hid under a bridge, where he was reported by a Mexican woman doing her wash. He, too, was found and killed.

Mexican Sgt. Felix Nuñez recalled one Texian who stood out:

> He was a tall American of rather dark complexion and had on a
> long buckskin coat and a round cap without any bill, made out of fox

Juan Morales
1802–1847

Juan Morales was born in Puebla, Mexico. During the Texas campaign, he commanded the battalion of San Luis Potosí. At the Alamo, Morales supervised construction of the earthworks around La Villita. In the final assault, Morales led the troops attacking the south wall and the wooden palisade near the chapel, which was defended by Davy Crockett and his Tennessee Mounted Volunteers.

After the Alamo battle, Morales was sent to join General Urrea's column of cavalry. He took part in the attack on Fannin's force at Coleto Creek and was one of the officers who negotiated Fannin's surrender. Morales was captured at San Jacinto and later supported General Urrea's opposition to General Filisola's decision to carry out Santa Anna's orders to leave Texas.

During the Mexican-American War, Morales commanded the Mexican garrison at Vera Cruz when it was attacked and captured by Gen. Winfield Scott's army. Morales was energetic, brave, and highly respected, and is sometimes referred to as "the brave Morales" in Mexican histories.

skin with the long tail hanging down his back. This man apparently had a charmed life. Of the many soldiers who took deliberate aim at him and fired, not one ever hit him. On the contrary, he never missed a shot. He killed eight of our men, besides wounding several others. This being observed by a lieutenant who had come in over the wall, he sprang at him and dealt him a deadly blow with his sword, just above the right eye, which felled him to the ground, and in an instant he was pierced by not less than twenty bayonets.

Captain Baugh gave the signal for the Texas men to hole up. The riflemen dropped down from the parapets and headed for the barracks.

The Texians dropped from the walls—Lt. George C. Kimble and the riders from Gonzales, Cleland Simmons and the dismounted cavalry, William Carey and the artillerymen of the west side. At the barracks, they entered rooms that had been prepared for a last-ditch defense: doorways blocked with parapets made of earth and topped with hides, parapets just high enough to rest a rifle. They sent off spurts of rifle fire from the parapets and from loopholes in the walls and doorways.

The Mexicans in the plaza ducked for cover, but there was no cover in this barren open space, and the soldiers fell everywhere.

The pressure on the north wall was so intense that the front ranks were boosted on to the top of the wall from below, and surged upward, to the point where bare timbers and wooden braces gave them a sort of ladder. Lt. José de la Peña described the scene:

> Officers of all ranks shouted orders. But were scarcely heard. The most daring of our veterans tried to be the first to climb, which they accomplished, yelling, sometimes climbing over the bodies of their comrades. Others, jammed together, made useless efforts, scrabbling in the dirt, obstructing others, and dying under the feet of the tramplers.
>
> From the roof of the barracks Texian riflemen fired down, scarcely able to miss in this roiling mass. The first of the climbers ran forward with bayonets to impale the defenders, rifles gave way to pistols and emptied pistols became clubs. The sharp reports of the rifles, the whistling of the bullets, the groans of the wounded, the surges of the men, the anguished cries of the dying, the arrogant harangues of the officers, the shouts of the attackers...bewildered all...the shouting of those being attacked was no less loud, and pierced our ears with

desperate terrible cries of alarm in a language we could not understand.

The mob surged forward and the defenders retreated before them, seeking shelter in the rooms on the east and west sides of the plaza. Gregorio Esparza had been assigned to one of the cannon on the east side of the plaza; he was

Gregorio Esparza
17??–1836

Gregorio Esparza was born into a well-to-do San Antonio family, but was captured by Comanche Indians as a child. He lived with them until he was a grown man, when he was ransomed. Later, he married Anita Salazár and they had five children.

Esparza joined with other Tejanos to fight with the Texians and participated in the battle of San Antonio under Juan Seguín. One of his brothers was a soldier in the Mexican Army, and when Santa Anna's army approached San Antonio, an officer advised Gregorio to take his family out of town. Because there were no carts available, he was delayed. A Texian friend came to the house while Gregorio was out and told Anita that Santa Anna was coming.

When Gregorio came home that day his wife asked him what he was going to do. "I am going to the fort..." he said.

"Then I am coming to the fort and so is the family," said Anita.

They spent the rest of the day moving their belongings by handcart and crossed the footbridge to the Alamo. As they moved the last of their goods, they could hear the sound of Santa Anna's army in the streets and the shot of a gun fired to announce the arrival of the troops. On that first night in the Alamo, Gregorio's unit went out and captured several Mexican prisoners. When the siege force closed in, Gregorio was assigned to one of the field guns and manned it until the end. He died at his gun from a stab wound in the side and a bullet in the head.

Of the Alamo defenders, his was the only body not burned; General Cós gave a special favor to Gregorio's brother who served in the Mexican Army. They removed Gregorio's body, took it to the cemetery, and buried it.

Toribio Domingo Losoya
1808=1836

Toribio Losoya was one of the Tejano heroes who died at the Alamo; he was born in the Alamo *barrio* and died there. Born in an old stone house in the southwest section of the mission compound, Losoya died in the chapel at the hands of Santa Anna's infantry.

The Losoyas were a San Antonio family of good repute and liberal persuasion. Toribio objected to Santa Anna's despotism and in the fall of 1835 he deserted the Mexican Army to enlist in Juan Seguín's company of Tejanos, participating in the capture of San Antonio.

His family was displaced when the Texas Army used their house and other buildings in the Alamo compound for nearly three months. When Santa Anna occupied San Antonio in February 1836, Losoya was one of seven Tejanos who went to the Alamo with their wives and children. Walter Lord wrote that Losoya was not in the Alamo on the day of the assault, but his body was identified by two residents of San Antonio in depositions in support of land claims.

found dead, slumped over his gun by the south window. Robert Evans kept the powder supply coming to Esparza as long as he could, but when Morales's men turned the eighteen-pounder about, all that ended and Esparza was bayoneted at his gun. Evans, wounded, grabbed a torch and headed for the powder room inside the chapel. He was about to blow the fort to kingdom come when he was stopped by the bullet that killed him.

Now only the chapel was left. Captain Dickinson's crew still manned the twelve-pounders on the high platform in back. He was joined by James Bonham.

Gregorio Esparza's family brought his body into the chapel but were followed by soldiers now out of control. Little Enrique Esparza was kneeling at his father's side when the soldiers burst in. Next to him was a young American boy, about twelve years old. The boy had been sleeping, but had awakened and covered himself with his blanket. The soldiers rushed at him. He offered no resistance as they skewered him with their bayonets and then cast his body aside to fall into the arms of little Enrique.

The sun still had not risen, but the brightening horizon lighted up the scene. The soldiers scrambling over the north wall were met by rifle fire from the defenders and also by friendly fire from Colonel Morales's men in the south end. The soldiers with bayonets ran around the plaza, stabbing the riflemen. The defenders fought back with clubbed rifles and bowie knives. Captain Dickinson went running into the chapel and found his wife.

"Great God, Sue! The Mexicans are inside our walls!" he shouted. "If they spare you, save my child." He kissed her, drew his sword, and disappeared. She never saw him again. He returned to his gun and

THE DEATH OF DICKINSON. OIL PAINTING BY THEODORE GENTILZ, 1896. THIS IMAGE COMES FROM AN ALBUMEN BOUDOIR CARD COPY OF THE PAINTING. *TEXAS STATE LIBRARY & ARCHIVES COMMISSION*

THE DESOLATE MONUMENT: LT. J. EDMUND BLAKE SKETCHED THE BATTLE-
SCARRED RUINS OF THE ALAMO GARRISON IN 1845.
TEXAS STATE LIBRARY & ARCHIVES COMMISSION

the ten other defenders. He was killed shortly afterward. Then James Bonham
fell, and the others, one by one.

Down at the south end, Colonel Morales's men used the eighteen-pound
cannon to begin blasting the Texas cannon and the doorways barricaded by the
Texas men. As the Mexican soldiers burst into the rooms where the Texians had
retreated, they fired indiscriminately, hitting both friend and foe.

"In this way our losses were most grievous," reported Lieutenant de la Peña.
He ought to have known; he was an officer in the elite Zapadores battalion of
crack combat engineers. "The tumult was great, the disorder frightful, as if the
furies had descended on us."

General Cós was finally persuaded that the carnage had to end to cut
Mexican losses. He ordered his bugler to blow the cease-fire. The bugler blew,
but no one paid any attention. The wild shooting continued even after the last
defender lay dead.

ELEVEN

❧

Inside the Walls

As the sun rose over the Alamo during the assault, the Mexican
soldiers had seen a strange blue flag hanging from a pole atop the long barracks.
It was the flag of the New Orleans Greys, and its legend read "God and Liberty."
Three sergeants of the Jimenez battalion had tried to get it down, and all three
had been cut down by gunfire. Then a sublieutenant of the Zapadores, José
María Torres, had run to the top of the barracks, pulled the flag down, and
raised Mexico's red, white, and green flag. The Alamo once more belonged to
Mexico.

A shot felled the officer who came to help Torres, and a second later another
dropped Torres. He died atop the blue flag.

In the same way that the Americans overwhelmed the Mexican defenders of
San Antonio in December, the Mexican soldiers now retaliated. First a blast
with a cannon to destroy the palisade in the doorway, then a volley of musketry
and a bayonet charge, shooting, tearing down walls, and knifing their way to
victory. Most of the killing occurred in the long barracks facing the plaza on the
east. Behind these walls the Texians stood and fired through a honeycomb of
loopholes. They had to be blasted out and then dealt with in hand-to-hand
combat. It took an hour to clear out the rooms of the old convent, and then the
chapel. Captain Dickinson's gunners had manned the twelve-pounders on the
high platform in the back until the end. De la Peña said that at the last, one of

the gunners seized a small child in his arms and leaped from the platform to his, and the child's, death.

Three unarmed gunners tried to take refuge in the chapel. The Mexican soldiers routed them out and killed them all. One, Jacob Walker, died an excruciating death. He ran into the sacristy, where Susannah Dickinson was sitting, daughter clutched to her bosom in her apron. Several of the soldiers bayoneted him, picked him up like a skewered cat, and tossed him up and down on their bayonets until he died, screaming for death. Susannah Dickinson caught a musket ball in the calf, but the wound was not serious.

In a room against the west wall, Juana Alsbury and her sister saw very little of the fighting. They peeped out and saw the columns of Santa Anna assaulting the defense from every side. They could hear the noises of battle, the pounding

ONCE SANTA ANNA'S ARMY HAD BREACHED THE WALLS OF THE ALAMO, FIERCE HAND-TO-HAND COMBAT ENSUED. THIS PHOTOENGRAVING OF THE FIGHTING IN THE BARRACKS ROOMS, *LAST STAND IN THE ALAMO*, SHOWS THE FINAL DESPERATE STRUGGLES OF THE DEFENDERS AS THE MEXICAN ARMY OVERWHELMS THEM. THIS IMAGE COMES FROM THE 1901 BOOK, *TEXAS HISTORY STORIES*.
TEXAS STATE LIBRARY & ARCHIVES COMMISSION

of the cannon, the splatter of the musketry, the groans of the wounded, and when it slowed, they knew that the defenders were being overwhelmed.

Juana asked her sister to go to the door and ask the Mexican soldiers not to fire into the room as there were only women inside. Señorita Gertrudis opened the door and was greeted by a torrent of abusive language. Her shawl was torn from her shoulders and she rushed back into the room. Juana stood nearby, clutching her baby to her breast and wondering if he would not be motherless soon.

The soldiers spoke. "Your money and your husband," they demanded.

"I have neither money nor husband," Gertrudis replied.

Eden Mitchell, a defender who was sick, rushed up and tried to protect Juana Alsbury. He was bayoneted at her side. A young Tejano grasped Juana's arm

Susannah Dickinson
1814=1883

Susannah Dickinson and her daughter Angelina were the only Anglo survivors of the Battle of the Alamo. Dickinson was the source of much information about the defenders of the Alamo, but it may not have always been accurate. As the years went on, her memory for details improved remarkably.

She was born in Tennessee and in 1829, when she was fifteen years old, she married Almeron Dickinson, a blacksmith. Two years later, the couple left Tennessee and settled near Gonzales in *empresario* Green DeWitt's Texas colony, where Susannah gave birth to their daughter, Angelina. In 1834, Almeron joined the Texas forces that captured San Antonio and the Alamo, while Susannah and Angelina stayed behind at Gonzales. They did not stay long; a few weeks later their home was looted by bandits and mother and daughter joined Almeron in San Antonio.

When Santa Anna approached in February 1836, the family moved to the Alamo. Susannah saw very little of the battle because she was confined to the sacristy of the chapel. She did see the deaths of several people, and she claimed that at the end Davy Crockett came into the sacristy, prayed, and then went out to face his death. Near the end, her husband came into the sacristy, embraced her, and then went back to man his cannon, where he fell a short time later. After the battle Susannah and her daughter went with Joe, William Travis's slave, and Ben, Colonel Almonte's black cook, to Gonzales, where she told the story of the fall of the Alamo to General Houston.

When Texas independence was won, Susannah applied for a government grant of $500, but it was denied. She married Francis Williams, but the marriage was not successful. Marrying three more times, she eventually moved to Austin with husband Joseph Hannig, a cabinetmaker. She died in 1883, having told her story many times and with many variations.

THE DEATH OF BOWIE, PAINTING BY LOUIS EYTH, 1878.
DAUGHTERS OF THE REPUBLIC OF TEXAS LIBRARY

and tried to keep her between himself and several assailants. They bayoneted him in the back, and several of them shot him.

The soldiers broke into the women's trunk and took money and clothes and some valuables that had been entrusted to them by defenders. A Mexican officer came up and asked them what they were doing there, and took them into the hall; he told them to stay where they were and he would take them to Santa Anna. Then Don Manuel Perez, the brother of Juana's first husband, came up calling, "Sister, sister!" They looked at him blankly.

"Don't you know your own brother-in-law ?" he asked

"I am so upset and distressed, I scarcely know anything," Juana said.

Don Manuel placed the women in charge of a slave belonging to Jim Bowie and they were taken to the house of Don Angel Navarro, where they were safe.

Some of the soldiers looted the rooms of other women who had sought sanctuary in the Alamo. The soldiers wandered about, stabbing and shooting the dead. They even killed a cat, saying, "This is not a cat but an American cat."

They found Jim Bowie on the south side of the chapel in the room where he was lying on a pallet, desperately ill. He had his pistols by his side. Legend

James Bowie
1796=1836

James Bowie, a legendary figure on the American frontier, was the son of legendary parents. It was said that when his father was arrested for killing a man, Bowie's mother and a slave broke into the jail and freed him.

Bowie was born in Georgia but grew up in Louisiana. After a sparse education he and his brothers entered the slave trade, from which they made a fortune. Their headquarters was New Orleans, a tough town where there were many fights, sometimes with knives. The famous Bowie knife which he and many other Alamo defenders used was actually invented by his brother, Rezin. James Bowie's reputation as a knife fighter grew out of an event in which he and an opponent had their trousers nailed together on a log and then went at each other with knives.

Bowie and his brothers dealt in stolen goods with the pirate Jean Lafitte, smuggled slaves, and went filibustering to Central America. In 1821 he joined an expedition into eastern Mexico. He liked San Antonio and moved there in 1828. After his marriage to Ursula Veramendi, the daughter of the governor of San Antonio, he went into land speculation and mining and made a fortune.

JAMES BOWIE, TEXAS SOLDIER WHO DIED DEFENDING THE ALAMO. TEXAS STATE LIBRARY & ARCHIVES COMMISSION

Granted Mexican citizenship by a special act of the Coahuila y Texas Legislature, Bowie qualified to buy eleven leagues (48,712 acres) of Texas land for about five cents per acre. Bowie then persuaded a number of Governor Veramendi's friends to apply for their eleven-league grants and to sell the titles to him. In a short time, Bowie had acquired 750,000 acres of Texas land. He became a respected citizen of San Antonio and was active in civic affairs.

In 1833 Bowie's wife and two children died in a cholera epidemic, after which he became active in the growing movement for the separation of Texas from Mexico. He was also deeply involved in the Texas land speculation of the 1830s, securing an appointment as a land commissioner and selling off thousands of acres of public lands for huge personal profit. When in 1834 General Cós appeared at Saltillo to straighten out the state's affairs, Bowie narrowly avoided jail. Responsible for the decision to defend the Alamo, he died there under Mexican guns.

has it that he began shooting as the Mexicans crashed into his room, though he may have been too sick to raise his head. One Mexican account says he cowered beneath his blanket. Judging from what we know of Bowie's character, this seems hard to believe.

They blew his brains out, firing so many shots his head matter stained the wall. Then they bayoneted the body repeatedly.

In the sacristy, Susannah Dickinson waited for the end. Gunner Anthony Wolfe's two young sons were bayoneted to death before her eyes as she crouched against the wall, daughter clutched in her apron. But the end did not come. She listened as the firing and the shouting died down. She was ordered to move from the sacristy to a little room just to the right of the main entrance. Presently Mrs. Esparza, her children, and the other women and children joined her there.

Suddenly a Mexican officer appeared in the room.

"Is Mrs. Dickinson here?" he asked in broken English.

She was too frightened to reply.

"Is Mrs. Dickinson here? Speak out. It's a matter of life and death."

"Yes," she answered.

"If you want to save your life, follow me."

She followed him outside the chapel, across the yard, past the long barracks. There was not much time for looking, but she saw many familiar figures crumpled on the ground, among them Davy Crockett, lying between the chapel and the long barracks, his "peculiar cap" beside him.

The story of Davy Crockett's end has been the subject of great controversy. Mrs. Dickinson claimed that he died in the plaza, firing his weapons until the last. He came to her in the chapel, she said, made his peace with God, and then went out and got killed. It must be noted that Susannah Dickinson was not a reliable witness. Her story changed over the years, and many historians have

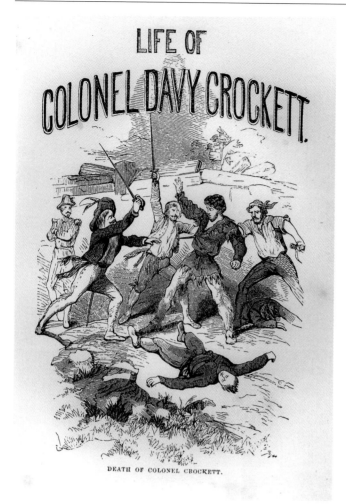

DEATH OF COLONEL CROCKETT.

DEATH OF COLONEL CROCKETT SHOWS THE FIGURE
UNARMED YET DEFIANT, AS A MEXICAN OFFICER CALM-
LY LOOKS ON. WOODCUT ILLUSTRATION FROM AN 1869
EDITION OF CROCKETT'S BIOGRAPHY.
TEXAS STATE LIBRARY & ARCHIVES COMMISSION

found her several stories incredible. More reliable is the testimony of one Mexican officer that he saw Crockett's body in the plaza, recognizing it by the coonskin cap Crockett wore at the Alamo. That story matches what we know of Davy Crockett's character as a brave and defiant figure. San Antonio Mayor Francisco Ruiz said he saw the body "in a little fort," probably the area in front of the chapel that Crockett and his men were defending, and that too indicates a death in action.

A much less flattering portrait of Crockett's death is given by de la Peña. According to him, half a dozen exhausted survivors were found hiding in a back room. Troops burst into the room and were eager to kill them. But Gen. Manuel Fernandez Castrillón came up and held the soldiers off. "Come with me to the general in chief and you will be saved," he said to the survivors. As he was a senior general, Santa Anna would listen to him, he told them. He escorted the prisoners to the general's presence. One of them, he said, was Davy Crockett. He described him. "The captive's face had gone far away with shock, but his cheeks were still red and his eyes were still blue. He was bent at the waist from dysentery, or maybe just from hunger."

But there was no hunger in the Alamo. They had enough provisions for a week or so. If anyone, it was the Mexicans who were hungry.

According to de la Peña's account, Crockett not only surrendered, but he lied about the fighting. He was a simple traveler who had been swept into the melée, he said. Castrillón presented the prisoners and asked for mercy.

"I do not want to see these men alive," Santa Anna said. "Take them out and shoot them."

There was some hesitation, then several of the officers who had not been involved in the fighting stepped forward and killed the prisoners with their swords.

José Enrique de la Peña
1807=1841

De la Peña was born in Jalisco, Mexico, in 1807 and was educated as a mining engineer before joining the Mexican Navy in 1825. He did not like Americans and once wrote a series of articles critical of the Mexican Navy, which was then commanded by Admiral David Porter, an American.

De la Peña met General Santa Anna in 1828 and joined his staff. In 1829, he fought in the battle of Tampico with Santa Anna against the Spanish. He then returned to naval duty, but when Santa Anna came to power in 1833, de la Peña secured a commission in the Mexican Army.

When the Texas Revolution broke out in 1835, de la Peña held a commission as a staff officer in the elite Zapadores battalion. During the Texas rebellion, he served as aide to Col. Francisco Duque of the Toluca battalion, arriving in San Antonio on March 4, 1836. During the battle of the Alamo he carried messages to and from the Toluca battalion, but that was his last participation in the war.

Afterwards, he testified in the court-martial of General Filisola for following Santa Anna's orders to withdraw from Texas, and he also wrote newspaper articles critical of Filisola. In 1837, de la Peña served in Sonora under Gen. José Urrea and took part in Urrea's uprising to support the Constitution of 1824; he was captured by government troops and imprisoned at Guadalajara. He was dishonorably discharged from the Mexican Army in 1839 and died in obscurity. He is notable for his history of the Texas Campaign, which claims that Davy Crockett surrendered at the Alamo to General Castrillón and was later executed by orders of Santa Anna. De la Peña's book is still the subject of controversy.

PHOTO OF SKETCH OF THE ALAMO AT THE END OF THE BATTLE. FRONTISPIECE
OF THE BOOK *SAN ANTONIO DE BÉXAR* BY MRS. S. J. WRIGHT, 1916.
TEXAS STATE LIBRARY & ARCHIVES COMMISSION

The problem with this story is that de la Peña did not know Davy Crockett
and did not claim to have seen him himself. The story reeks of iconoclasm man-
ufactured after the fact. It does not square with Crockett's known character or
what is known of his brief stay in Texas. The image projected was that of a
frightened old man, and Crockett at forty-nine was neither old nor frightened.
Other Mexican eyewitnesses later told of several survivors executed, but it seems
doubtful that Davy Crockett was one of them.

It was all over by 6:30 in the morning. The Mexicans were no longer shooting or bayoneting the bodies. The Alamo was quiet, and the fires that had been
kindled here and there were burning down. Santa Anna ordered the slave Joe to
identify the bodies of Travis, Bowie, and Crockett. (If he had seen Crockett executed before his eyes, would he have needed him identified minutes later?) He
then called the troops into a hollow square in the plaza for a speech. He praised
the soldiers and thanked them in the name of Mexico.

Except for Mrs. Dickinson, the women were confined with their children
in the southeast room of the chapel. The women were not molested, although it

was a very near thing. Some of the soldiers cast longing eyes, but the officers intervened.

The Battle of the Alamo ended. An army of 1,500 Mexicans had overrun a defense of 183. General Santa Anna had said "No Quarter" and there was no quarter.

"It was but a small affair," General Santa Anna told Capt. Fernando Urizza that day. The general had no idea of the implications of this small battle. As William Barret Travis had said on the eve of battle:

> I feel confident that the determined valour and desperate courage, heretofore evinced by my men, will not fail them in the last struggle, and although they may be sacrificed to the vengeance of a Gothic enemy, the victory will cost the enemy so dear, that it will be worse for him than a defeat.

But at the moment the Mexicans were jubilant in victory. The bodies of the slain Texians and Tejanos were stripped, and their valuables divided among the soldiers. Later in the day the women and children were marched from the chapel through the piles of dead Mexicans, dead Texians, and dead Tejanos, then they were escorted across the footbridge and into San Antonio. They were taken to the house of a loyal Mexican family and there they were fed and cared for. Santa Anna gave them individual audiences and money. Gregorio Esparza's widow was one of the women.

Then *El Presidente* dealt with Susannah Dickinson. He offered to adopt her

PHOTO OF THE BIBLE BELONGING TO COLONEL TRAVIS. IT WAS FOUND IN THE ALAMO AFTER THE BATTLE.
TEXAS STATE LIBRARY & ARCHIVES COMMISSION

daughter and when she refused the honor he gave her two pesos and a blanket, and she went off with her story of the fall of the Alamo.

Santa Anna then summoned *Alcalde* (mayor) Ruiz and demanded that the city authorities take care of the bodies of the dead. The Mexican soldiers would be buried in the Campo Santo Cemetario. But what about the Texians and Tejanos? The rebels were infidels, he said, thus dismissing the conversion to the Catholic faith of Jim Bowie and others. Their bodies should be burned. The single exception was the body of Gregorio Esparza, whose brother was a soldier in the Mexican Army. General Cós had intervened and Gregorio's body was picked up by three of his brothers and buried in consecrated ground.

According to Ruiz:

> Santa Anna, after all the Mexicans were taken out ordered wood to be brought to burn the bodies of the Texans. He sent a company of dragoons with me to bring wood and dry branches from the neighboring forest. About three o'clock in the afternoon they commenced laying the wood and dry branches upon which a pile of dead bodies was placed; more wood was piled on them, and another pile brought, and in this manner they were arranged in layers. Kindling wood was distributed through the pile, and about five o'clock in the evening it was lighted.
>
> The dead Mexicans of Santa Anna were taken to the graveyard, but not having sufficient room for them, I ordered them to be thrown into the river, which was done that same day.
>
> Santa Anna's loss was estimated at sixteen hundred men. These were the flower of his army.
>
> The gallantry of the few Texans who defended the Alamo was really wondered at by the Mexican army. Even the generals were astonished at their vigorous resistance, and how dearly victory was brought.

A local teenager watched the bodies burning and later remembered, "I saw an immense pillar of fire shoot up south and east of the Alamo, and dense smoke from it rose high into the clouds." The stink from the burning flesh dominated the atmosphere for two days.

After Susannah Dickinson refused the offer of adoption for her daughter she set out for Gonzales. They were accompanied by Travis's slave Joe and Ben, Colonel Almonte's servant. Santa Anna wanted the word of the Alamo—and its message—spread throughout Texas.

On March 11, Gen. Sam Houston, just back from negotiating a treaty with

THE BURNING OF THE BODIES OF THE SLAIN DEFENDERS OF THE ALAMO.
SKETCH BY LEO COTTON.
TEXAS STATE LIBRARY & ARCHIVES COMMISSION

the Comanches, rode into Gonzales accompanied by a hundred men. Houston's first news about the fate of the Alamo came from two Tejanos who arrived in town that afternoon bearing word that all the defenders of the Alamo had been slain, as were several hundred Mexican soldiers as well.

That night General Houston wrote to Colonel Fannin at Goliad:

> On my arrival here this afternoon, the following intelligence was received through a Mexican…Anselmo Bergara states that he left the Alamo on Sunday, the 6th inst;…that the Alamo was attacked on Sunday morning at the dawn of day, by about two thousand three hundred men, and carried a short time before sunrise, with the loss of five hundred and twenty-one Mexicans killed and as many wounded. Colonel Travis had only one hundred and fifty effective men out of his entire force of one hundred eighty seven. After the fort was carried, seven men surrendered, and called for Santa Anna and quarter. They were murdered by his order. Colonel Bowie was sick in bed, and also

murdered. The enemy expect a reinforcement of fifteen hundred men...and a reserve of fifteen hundred to follow...

I have little doubt that the Alamo has fallen... In corroboration of the truth of the fall of the Alamo, I have ascertained that Colonel Travis intended firing signal guns at three different periods of each day until succor should arrive. No signal guns have been heard since Sunday, though a scouting party have just returned who approached within twelve miles of it, and remained there forty-eight hours.

Accompanying that letter was an order to Colonel Fannin:

You will, as soon as practical after receipt of this order, fall back upon Guadalupe Victoria, with your command, and such artillery as can be brought with expedition. The remainder will be sunk in the river. You takes [sic] the necessary measures for the defense of Victoria, and forward one third the number of your effective men to this point, and remain in command until further orders.

Every facility is to be afforded to women and children who may be desirous of leaving that place. Previous to abandoning Goliad, you will take the necessary measures to blow up that fortress; and do so before leaving its vicinity. The immediate advance of the enemy may be confidently expected, as well as a rise of water. Prompt movements are therefore highly important.

On the following day General Houston created the 1st Texas Volunteer Regiment and put Edward Burleson in command. Burleson accepted his demotion from general to colonel with equanimity. He was a soldier, and knew how to take orders.

Two days later, on Sunday, March 13, Houston dispatched his most trusted scout, Deaf Smith, to go west and confirm the Alamo story. On the way Smith encountered Susannah Dickinson and her companions and brought them back to Gonzales. Ben carried a message from Santa Anna to all Tejanos calling on them to return to the Mexican fold. The message for the Texians was the widowhood of Susannah Dickinson. The *norteamericanos* could expect nothing but death if they persisted in their revolution.

TWELVE

⌘

The Runaway Scrape

The message to the Texians brought instant panic. Every inhabitant of Gonzales picked up his most precious possessions and headed east. By dawn Gonzales was deserted. As the refugees moved eastward, they saw the sky behind them turn red and the air fill with the sound of explosions; Gen. Sam Houston had put Gonzales to the torch.

Later, the Texians would refer to this ruefully as the Runaway Scrape, but at the moment sheer panic ruled in the realization that General Santa Anna's army was just days away.

General Houston did not waste any time on recrimination. Jim Bowie and Colonel Neill had defied his orders, but Bowie was dead, and Neill now seemed more tranquil. The defense of the Alamo had been a military blunder, but so had Santa Anna's No Quarter policy, and a catchphrase in honor of the brave defenders was on everyone's lips.

Remember The Alamo.

Militarily, there was a lesson here: Travis had let his men be "forted up," a tragic error Sam Houston had learned from in the Creek War, when the Indians did the same and were wiped out.

TEXAS!!

Emigrants who are desirious of assist-
ing Texas at this important crisis of her
affairs may have a free passage and equip-
ments, by applying at the
NEW-YORK and PHILADELPHIA HOTEL,
On the Old Levee, near the Blue Stores.

Now is the time to ensure a fortune in Land:
To all who remain in Texas during the War will
be allowed 1280 Acres.
To all who remain Six Months, 640 Acres.
To all who remain Three Months, 320 Acres.
And as Colonists, 4600 Acres for a family and
1470 Acres for a Single Man.
New Orleans, April 23d, 1836.

BROADSIDE ADVERTISING TEXAS LANDS ISSUED JUST BEFORE THE FALL OF THE
ALAMO.
CENTER FOR AMERICAN HISTORY, UNIVERSITY OF TEXAS AT AUSTIN

"Our forces must not be shut up in forts, where they can neither be provided with men nor provisions," he said. "Long aware of this fact, I directed on
the 16th of January last that the artillery should be removed and
the Alamo blown up, but it was prevented by the expedition
upon Matamoros, the author of all our misfortunes."

At the moment Texas's future looked very grim.
General Houston had only 375 men with two days'
rations, a few very poor horses, two wagons, and two
yoke of oxen to pull them. He faced a 3,000-man army
which his spies said was moving against him at the
rate of twenty-five miles a day. But something could
be done about that. Santa Anna's animals needed

GEN. SAM HOUSTON, WHO LED THE TEXAS ARMY IN THE
DESPERATE DAYS FOLLOWING THE ALAMO'S FALL TO
SANTA ANNA. PAINTING BY EDWARD SCHNABEL.
GREGORY'S OLD MASTER GALLERY

José Domingo Losoya
1783=1869

Another member of the Losoya family, José Losoya was born a Spanish subject but fled Mexico after the battle of Medina in 1813. He went to Louisiana, where he enlisted in the United States Army and fought under Gen. Andrew Jackson at the Battle of New Orleans in 1815. He remained in the U.S. until the success of the Mexican revolution in 1820, when he returned to San Antonio and married.

In Texas, José Losoya joined Captain Seguín's cavalry company in 1835 and served under Col. James Bowie in the battle of Concepción. In the attack on San Antonio, he captured the Garza house on the plaza. Joining General Houston's staff at Gonzales, he served as a forage master, a sort of quartermaster general. He fought at the Battle of San Jacinto and was afterwards given a land grant which became his home ranch at Losoya, where he died.

grass, and the Texians could deny it to them by burning the fields. Scorched earth became the policy of the Texas Army.

Domingo Losoya, the forage master, was instructed to secure the feed for the Texas Army's animals and to destroy all the rest. Nature gave a hand by bringing in the rainy season; the roads were turned into soup and the fields into quagmires as floods spread across the flatlands of the river bottoms.

By March 15, Houston's force had reached the Navidad River and was increasing every day as men joined the colors. He had no word from Fannin.

March 15 was also the day the Texas government at Washington-on-the-Brazos learned of the fall of the Alamo, and panic set in there, too. Two days later the convention adjourned and the delegates dispersed. The government fled. The cabinet traveled together and at night the high officials slept on the floor, the secretary of the navy and the attorney general sharing a blanket.

The shopkeepers packed up too. At the river crossings, thousands of people waited for the ferries which came jammed to overflowing. No one knew to what lengths Santa Anna might go. The stories circulated: The Mexicans had sold poisoned food to the Alamo defenders, thus weakening them for the slaughter. Prisoners had been castrated and other indignities inflicted on them.

The army reached Burnam's Ferry on the Colorado River, and there was talk of making a stand there. But in the end Houston vetoed the idea; the threat of being surrounded and cut off was too great. They crossed the river on March 17, and turned south. On March 19, Houston set up camp at Beason's Landing on the east bank. The army had grown to 600 men but he needed more. If Fannin would abandon Goliad and bring his men to the coast, and Houston could link up with the 200 men at Matagordo, he would begin to have a respectable army.

But Fannin seems to have been paralyzed by the disasters that had struck Johnson and Grant. He sat at Goliad. He wasted time arguing with the local settlers to get them moving. Fannin also made the error of dividing his command. He sent Capt. Amon King to Refugio to organize the settlers for evacuation. But King exceeded his orders and undertook to punish several Tejano families that had taken Santa Anna's advice and gone back into the Mexican fold. The punitive expedition delayed him, and when he returned to Refugio he was surrounded by Urrea's cavalry. Fannin learned of this on March 12, the day that he received Houston's order to retreat. So cocksure of himself before, Fannin now became hesitant.

Bravery or Blunder?

Did the heroes of the Alamo know what they were doing or were they victims of a great military blunder?

General Houston sent Col. Jim Bowie to San Antonio with orders to blow up the Alamo and move the guns to Goliad. But when Bowie got there and saw what Lieutenant Colonel Neill had done to improve the military quality of the place, he changed his mind. But General Houston was right: Santa Anna's Mexican Army of more than 3,000 men would have overwhelmed the defenders even if their number had been increased by the 350 men of Goliad. As Houston knew, to be "forted up" was suicidal for the tiny Texas Army.

In any event, the courageous stand of this handful of brave men created a stirring catchphrase: Remember the Alamo! Hundreds of Texians and Americans heeded this call to arms, and Texas was soon made free.

"We could not remember ever having seen Fannin, usually so gallant and at times almost rash, so undecided," said Herman Ehrenberg, the youngest of the New Orleans Greys. Fannin sent Col. William Ward of the Georgia battalion and 200 of his troops to extricate King and his men. Ward arrived at Refugio just after Urrea's cavalry had destroyed the King group. The cavalry chased the Texians into Refugio, then attacked. Ward tried to escape with his men in a driving rainstorm but had to leave his wounded. General Urrea now had more than fifty prisoners, and orders from Santa Anna to execute all of them. This Urrea was reluctant to do, although his officers were pressing him to relieve the burden of guarding them. Finally he acceded to their requests. On March 16, Urrea's men executed thirty prisoners in the plaza at Refugio.

That same day, Fannin called an officers council. The council advised immediate retreat, as General Houston had ordered. But it was too late. Urrea's cavalry came up and attacked his outposts. Fannin ordered the artillery dismounted and buried. Then he changed his mind, and the artillery was dug up. Once again, Fannin changed his mind and said he would retreat. On the morning of March 18, the retreat began. Spying a small group of Mexican cavalry in the distance, Col. Albert C. Horton led the Fannin cavalry out to do battle, not knowing that this was part of a larger unit. Horton's men were chased back into the *presidio*, where they arrived exhausted. The retreat was postponed one day. That night was rainy and cold, another blue norther. Fannin burned all the stores he could not carry and demolished much of the fortress. At 9 A.M. on the 19th, Fannin and his men slipped out of Goliad under cover of dense fog and set out for Victoria.

At about noon, a Mexican cavalry patrol entered the deserted fortress. General Urrea learned that his birds had flown and set out in pursuit.

"I desired to obtain a triumph for our nation on this day," he said, "to celebrate my birthday—pardon my personal pride."

Fannin had already shown that his judgment was not worthy of a senior officer in anybody's army. The manner of his retreat confirmed all of Sam Houston's doubts: The Fannin column had too much artillery, too many personal possessions, very little food and water, and no forage for the animals. After two hours, the fog burned off and the hot Texas sun beat down on them. At the first river crossing, they found the banks so steep that the men had to unload and then reload some of the carts. By midafternoon, the men and animals were exhausted, although they had traveled only seven miles.

Fannin called a halt, and the oxen were unyoked before freeing them to graze. Colonel Horton had four scouts out for the column; they claimed that the

Mexicans were five miles behind and did not seem inclined to attack. Having reported, the colonel's men stopped off for a siesta. The oxen were grazed, yoked again, and hitched to the wagons. After two miles, the oxen began to give out. They had reached a hollow about a mile from the sheltering forest of Coleto Creek. When Fannin gave the order to make camp, his officers objected. It would be much better, they said, to go on to Coleto Creek, where the thick woods would give them shelter. Fannin said no, they would stop here, and they did. The cavalry scouts were awakened by the sound of hoofbeats and sprang into their saddles just in time to avoid being trampled by the Mexican cavalry. They fled past Fannin's men, and the Mexicans were soon upon the column.

First the Mexican cavalry charged and were repelled. Then the infantry came up with fixed bayonets. This charge, too, was sent reeling. The air was so humid the Texian gunpowder got damp and useless. Some of the men went among the bodies of the dead and wounded, searching for weapons loaded with dry powder. Fannin brought out his artillery and the Texians met the bayonet charges with volleys of grapeshot. At any moment, Fannin expected Colonel Horton to come to the rescue with the cavalry. They never came.

General Urrea then decided to let the Texas sun do the job, and he backed off. During the long afternoon, the Mexican snipers kept up a harassing fire. The list of Texian wounded grew, including Colonel Fannin, who was hit in the thigh. By nightfall the wounded were crying for water, but there was none.

The Mexicans stood off that night, firing occasionally just to show that they were still there. Fannin did not know that the Mexicans were short of ammunition.

Fannin's officers reviewed their situation. Nine men had been killed and fifty-one wounded. They did not know how many casualties the Mexicans had suffered (fifty-one killed and a hundred and forty wounded). They did know that their food was almost exhausted and their ammunition was low. The oxen were all dead, which meant no transportation for the wounded. Sniper fire throughout the night indicated that Urrea had them surrounded. The able-bodied might escape if they left under the cover of night, but the wounded had no way out. Typically, the indecisive Fannin posed the question to his officers: "What shall we do?"

They decided to stay with the wounded and share their fate. The able-bodied worked all night to prepare earthworks, but on the morning of March 19 they had more bad news: During the night, General Urrea had received reinforcements. He now had more than a thousand men and several cannon against the two hundred effective Texians. The Texian situation was hopeless.

THE MARCH TO THE MASSACRE, OIL PAINTING BY COL. ANDREW J. HOUSTON (SAM HOUSTON'S SON). PHOTO BY CECIL THOMPSON. *TEXAS STATE LIBRARY & ARCHIVES COMMISSION*

Fannin ran up a white flag. The Mexicans ran up a white flag of their own and Fannin, limping, led a delegation out to discuss terms of surrender with the three Mexican delegates. There would be no terms, General Urrea said. He did not have the authority to negotiate.

"If you gentlemen wish to surrender at discretion, the matter is ended. Otherwise I shall return to my camp and renew the attack."

Fannin's men were exhausted. Fannin chose to sign the surrender document. Colonel Horton arrived with what remained of his cavalry, and reinforcements from Victoria, who totalled fewer than forty men. They looked at the scene, listened to the Mexican bugles blowing, and turned and galloped away toward Victoria. They would live to fight another day.

It appeared that General Urrea was going to be generous. His men brought water and cared for the wounded. The Americans had two doctors, Joseph Henry Barnard and Jack Shackelford, and they worked in a tent with the Mexican doctors, treating the wounded indiscriminately.

Many of the prisoners believed they were going to be paroled, and the volunteers from America joked among themselves about going home.

At about two o'clock in the afternoon, the rebels were herded back into the Goliad *presidio* and imprisoned in the burned-out chapel, joining others who had been captured by Urrea's army. These included Colonel Ward and 120 of his Georgia battalion who had tried to rescue Captain King. They had escaped Mexican encirclement and met with Fannin, then wandered about for a week trying to reach Victoria. Then they had run up against another superior force of

Urrea's cavalry. The prisoners also included eighty-two fresh volunteers from New York who had stepped off their ship at Copano into Mexican arms.

It took two more days to bring the wounded in by cart. In the meantime there was much talk about parole, and much trading with the Mexican soldiers, swapping clothing for tortillas. The *norteamericanos* did not know it, but they were under sentence of death by Santa Anna, and General Urrea was doing everything he could to circumvent the disaster.

Urrea failed to achieve clemency for the prisoners. Santa Anna wrote a letter to the officer in charge of the prisoners, demanding their immediate execution.

Urrea also wrote, telling the officer not to execute the prisoners. The two letters arrived on Saturday night, March 26. The officer decided to follow the orders of *El Presidente*. The prisoners awoke on the morning of Palm Sunday, March 27, to discover that the cannon aimed at the front gate had been turned around to aim at them. Soldiers with lighted torches stood behind each gun, which was packed with grapeshot. At eight o'clock, between 425 and 445 prisoners were assembled, divided into three columns, and marched off in three different directions, guarded by Mexican soldiers.

The Greys and a few others were marched toward Victoria. They thought they were going to a port to be shipped back to New Orleans. The Georgia battalion was marched off on one branch of the trail and Fannin's militia on another. Then it was murder in triplicate. Each column was halted, the prisoners were ordered to kneel, and the Mexican soldiers shot them to death.

Herman Ehrenberg survived the horror. He was with the Greys on the road to Victoria. After about fifteen minutes of marching, they were turned off to the left toward the San Antonio River, which threaded through the spring grassland. He noticed several troops of cavalry carrying their long lances. The prisoners were led toward a high mesquite hedge, and the Mexican soldiers formed a double file behind them. A Mexican officer shouted at the prisoners to halt.

Ehrenberg recalled:

> At that moment we heard the muffled rolling of a musket volley in the distance. Involuntarily we thought of our companions, who had been separated from us and evidently led off in that direction.
>
> Astonished and confounded, we looked at each other and cast questioning glances, first at ourselves and then at the Mexicans. Then another command rang out—Kneel down—from the lips of the Mexican officers. Only a few of us understood Spanish and could not or would not obey the order.

Meanwhile the Mexican soldiers, who were barely three steps away, had leveled their muskets at our chests and we found ourselves in terrible surprise.

We still considered it impossible to believe that they were going to shoot us...With threatening gestures and drawn sword the chief of the murderers for the second time commanded in a brusque tone, "Kneel down."

A second volley thundered over to us from another direction, and a confused cry, probably from those who were not immediately killed, accompanied it.

Someone cried out: "Comrades, listen to that crying. It means our brothers! Hear their cry! It is their last one! There is no more hope— the last hour of the Greys has come! Therefore—Comrades!"

A terrible cracking interrupted him, and then everything was quiet. A thick smoke slowly rolled toward the San Antonio. The blood of my lieutenant was on my clothing and around me quivered my friends...I did not see more. I jumped up quickly, concealed by the black smoke of the powder, and rushed down the hedge to the river.

In the Goliad *presidio* the wounded prisoners were taken outside and shot, and those who could not walk were transported by cart. The wounded were all shot, bayoneted, or sabred to death, and their bodies were all burned.

Colonel Fannin came out of his room and asked what was going on. Mexican Capt. Carolino Huerta directed him to a place near the chapel wall. Limping, Fannin approached the wall. He gave the officer a gold watch and asked that the officer guarantee his burial. The captain bowed. Then Fannin gave the captain a purse containing ten pesos and asked that he not be shot in the head. The captain took the purse. Fannin was blindfolded, then sat down on the chair provided for him. At Huerta's command, the firing squad shot Fannin in the head. His body was cast on the common heap and burned.

A few survived the massacre. The doctors and medical orderlies, the eighty-two New York innocents who had not fired a shot on Texas soil, some carpenters, and others the Mexicans found useful were spared. Twenty-eight other prisoners, including Herman Ehrenberg, escaped and survived to tell the story of the massacre twice as great as that at the Alamo. The Texians now had two battle cries:

Remember the Alamo!

Remember Goliad!

THE INTERIOR OF THE BATTLE-SCARRED CHURCH OF THE ALAMO GARRISON.
TEXAS STATE LIBRARY & ARCHIVES COMMISSION

The massacre shocked the most hardened professionals of Santa Anna's army. Many of the officers at Goliad could not eat their dinners that night; some of them cried openly. General Urrea learned of it only after it had been done. Lieutenant de la Peña cogently summed up the effect:

> So many and such cold-blooded murders tarnished our glory, took away the fruits of victory, and would prolong the war and make its success doubtful, because it provoked the enemy and placed him in the difficult position of vanquishing or dying.

General Houston's ragged army was at Beason's Landing on March 19, when Fannin surrendered his force at Coleto Creek; Houston was still there two days later when General Sesma and his army reached the river across from him and camped. A few days later, Sesma was joined by the smaller force of Gen. Eugenio Tolsa, and there they sat glaring across the raging Colorado River, waiting for the flood to subside so they could cross. On the other side, the Army of Texas was spoiling for a fight, and the officers urged Houston to attack. They were eager to avenge the massacred men at the Alamo.

Disillusionment had set in and Houston did nothing to stop it. Burned by past experience, he kept his own counsel and did not respond to the men's complaints and jeers.

Through his scout Deaf Smith, Houston knew that he was being trailed by three separate forces: General Urrea in the south, General Gaona in the north, and General Sesma in the center. If he engaged any one of them, the other two would soon be there. The only strategy with any chance of success was to retreat until he had the enemy where he wanted them—deep in the heart of the Texas bottomlands, far from the supply center at San Antonio.

Houston was at Beason's when he learned of Fannin's surrender at Coleto Creek. He had already given up on Fannin. "If what I have heard be true," he said, "I deplore it and can only attribute the ill luck to his attempting to retreat in daylight in the face of a superior force. He is an ill-fated man." How ill-fated, Sam Houston did not yet know.

What he did know was that his fellow Texians were looking to him to save them as they fled before the Mexican Army. As he had moved east, he found nothing but signs of panic. In the houses doors stood open, beds were unmade, uneaten breakfasts were still on the tables, unwashed dishes still in the sinks, pans of milk moldering in the dairies. The cribs were full of corn, the smokehouses full of bacon and hams hanging down from the rafters, the yards full of chickens cackling and scratching for food, nests of eggs in every corner, young corn and garden truck soaked by the rain. In the fields, cattle were grazing in the luxuriant stands of grass and hogs wallowed comfortably in the mud puddles. All this had been abandoned.

But as they fled, the Texians were burning with resentment and determination. The Mexicans would pay.

THIRTEEN

❧

On the March

Before my God, since we parted I have found the darkest hours of my life," General Houston wrote Secretary of War Rusk on March 25. He had just learned of the surrender and massacre of Fannin's Goliad group, and knew that he could not count on those five hundred men to swell his slender army. He realized that his army was the last hope of Texas, and that he could not commit it against unfavorable odds, so although he had promised the army a battle at Beason's there could be no battle. He ordered the retreat again to San Felipe, and when they got there on March 28, he told his men that the next day they would continue the march to Groce's Plantation on the Brazos.

With that announcement 200 men deserted, loudly proclaiming their disgust with a general who would not fight. Houston was dismayed, but he stuck to his guns. He did not call an officers council and he did not explain; he bore the weight of command alone. The next day the army marched again, leaving behind two companies whose commanders refused to move. Capt. Mosely Baker insisted on defending San Felipe, and Capt. Wiley Martin said he would defend the Fort Bend crossing. Houston ordered them to do what they were going to do anyhow, then marched twenty miles to the north, to Groce's. The wisdom of his course was soon shown; General Tolsa's force joined up with General Sesma and made camp opposite Beason's, waiting for the foaming Colorado to subside so they could cross. Had Houston remained on the

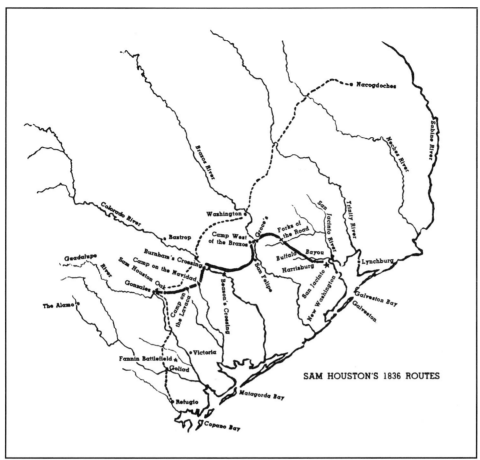

A MAP OF GEN. SAM HOUSTON'S ROUTES DURING THE DECISIVE CAMPAIGNS OF TEXAS'S WAR OF INDEPENDENCE FROM MEXICO.
UT INSTITUTE OF TEXAN CULTURES AT SAN ANTONIO

Colorado River, he would have been attacked by this combined superior force.

As the army splashed and struggled in the mud, General Houston tried to raise the spirits of the men. "My friends," he told them, "ill-disposed persons have told you that I am going to march you to the redlands [badlands]. This is false. I am going to lead you to the Brazos Bottom to a position where you can whip the enemy even if he comes ten to one and where we can get an abundant supply of corn."

But many of the soldiers remained unconvinced. They had retreated and retreated and they were retreating again.

When the news of Fannin's surrender reached General Santa Anna, he thought the rebellion was ended. The Alamo had fallen, Gonzales had been burned, the settlers were fleeing, and the Texas Army was leading the flight. All that was needed, it seemed, was mopping up, and that was no job for the commander in chief, who had other worries on his mind. Miguel Barragán, the man Santa Anna had installed as stand-in president, had died on March 1, and his successor had already issued a decree overturning Santa Anna's policy of no quarter for rebels. It was time to get back to Mexico City and reestablish his authority.

But when Santa Anna announced his decision to leave, several of his generals objected. One of them suggested that the Mexican Army might even be defeated. But the most telling point was that General Urrea was stealing Santa Anna's thunder. "Urrea does everything," one soldier observed, "while we just sit and watch."

Santa Anna pricked up his ears at that; he had a wonderfully developed sense of survival. He would resume active command. One other problem was brought up. The Mexican supply line was too long, and the supplies were running out. That was all right, said Santa Anna, the army would live off the country.

Once the decision was made, Santa Anna moved quickly. On April 4, he reached the combined Sesma-Tolsa force. The next day he forced them to cross the river and moved to San Bernardo Creek, thirteen miles north. At two o'clock on the morning of April 6, Santa Anna led 300 men to attack San Felipe. They found the place in ashes. The town had been burned by Captain Baker, who had retreated across the Colorado. Santa Anna brought up two field pieces and shelled the breastworks Baker's men had built. A Mexican patrol captured one of Baker's pickets, who said that Houston had retreated to Groce's Plantation. Santa Anna believed he had finally treed his enemy.

On April 9, Santa Anna left the main force and took a flying column of 700 men to go after Houston. On April 12 they reached Thompson's Ferry on the Brazos, near Fort Bend, and through a clever ruse, succeeded in capturing the ferry. Colonel Almonte, who had been educated in America, spoke colloquial American English. He called the ferryman, who thought he was a Texas officer and brought the ferry. The ferryman was subdued, and the ferry was Santa Anna's. He now had a way to cross into Houston's territory. At Fort Bend, Santa Anna gained intriguing information: The rebel government had left Washington and was at Harrisburg, thirty miles away. If Santa Anna could capture the government, the rebellion would collapse. He would hang them all, especially Lorenzo de Zavala, that traitor to Mexico.

At Groce's Plantation the Army of Texas stopped to rest. Jared E. Groce was a rich man, and he turned his plantation over to the army; his mansion became a hospital, his blacksmith shop an armory, and his servants fed the army from the gardens and the herds.

In spite of desertions, the Texas Army now numbered 900 men. They rested at the plantation for two weeks, during which time General Houston gave them some elementary discipline; they received supplies from Harrisburg, including two cannon named the Twin Sisters.

With the two weeks of rest, the morale of the army improved, but from Harrisburg came repercussions. President David G. Burnet had no use for Houston, so he sent Secretary Rusk to Groce's with a stinging letter:

> Sir. The enemy are laughing you to scorn. You must fight them. You must retreat no further. The country expects you to fight. The salvation of the country depends on your doing so.

So negative was the government attitude toward Houston that Rusk had been authorized to assume command. Wisely, he refrained from doing so.

On April 12, General Houston ordered his refreshed army to march. He had acquired the services of the steamboat *Yellow Stone,* whose Captain Ross had agreed to transport the army across the Brazos River. In several trips over the next two days, the boat brought the army across. Then they headed east, but where they were going only Houston knew, and he kept his own counsel.

Santa Anna was marching too, against Harrisburg, where he hoped to capture the Texas government. When he reached Harrisburg, he discovered that the cabinet had fled to New Washington, and was planning to escape to Galveston Island. He sent Colonel Almonte with fifty dragoons to intercept; he also discovered that Houston had left Groce's Plantation and was heading east, though this did not worry him. Santa Anna was convinced that Houston would not fight. Houston, he was told, was escorting

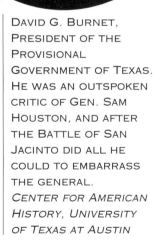

DAVID G. BURNET, PRESIDENT OF THE PROVISIONAL GOVERNMENT OF TEXAS. HE WAS AN OUTSPOKEN CRITIC OF GEN. SAM HOUSTON, AND AFTER THE BATTLE OF SAN JACINTO DID ALL HE COULD TO EMBARRASS THE GENERAL. *CENTER FOR AMERICAN HISTORY, UNIVERSITY OF TEXAS AT AUSTIN*

Sam Houston
1793≠1863

"REMEMBER THE ALAMO"

As a young man, Sam Houston lived with the Cherokee and he never forgot it; his favorite costume was a pair of buckskin trousers and a Cherokee hunting shirt. He loved to drink, and it was said that in San Felipe during the Constitutional Convention he and Jim Bowie were drunk together every night. During the military campaign he cut down on his drinking, but used to sniff from a vial a substance his enemies said was opium but his friends said was hartshorn (ammonia). He had a large capacity for making friends, and an even larger one for making enemies, who never let up their attacks on his actions and character.

After serving under Andrew Jackson in the Creek War, Houston remained in the army for several years, then resigned his commission and went to Tennessee to study law. He successfully ran for Congress, serving from 1823 until 1827. When his friend Andrew Jackson was elected President, he became an intimate of the White House. He was then elected governor of Tennessee, only to resign suddenly and leave the state two years later after a mysterious altercation with his bride of a few weeks, who returned to the paternal hearth.

Houston hated sham and showed it. One night in Washington at a diplomatic reception he encountered a fop of a Frenchman with a chestful of honorary medals. Houston was dressed in his usual diplomatic costume: buckskin leggings and a Cherokee blanket. He

SAM HOUSTON WEARS A COWBOY DUSTER IN THIS DAGUERREOTYPE.
TEXAS STATE LIBRARY & ARCHIVES COMMISSION

observed the Frenchman's medals for a moment, and then swept aside his blanket to reveal his broad chest crisscrossed with battle scars from the Creek War. "Monsieur," he said, "a humble citizen soldier salutes you."

Self-educated in the classics and well-trained in the military, Houston rose to the rank of general in the Tennessee militia. Eventually, he settled in Texas and became a delegate from Nacogdoches to the Convention of 1833. From the outset of the Texas Revolution, he had a strategic vision of wearing the enemy down and ultimately defeating him on ground of Houston's own choosing, which is what happened at San Jacinto.

Following the revolution, Houston was elected President of the Republic of Texas and after annexation he represented Texas in the United States Senate. He was governor of Texas when the state seceded and joined the Confederacy in 1861, but he refused to endorse the secession, which brought about his removal from office. His children sided with the secessionists and deserted him.

SAM HOUSTON AFTER THE TEXAS REVOLUTION. ENGRAVING BY GEORGE E. PERINE. *TEXAS STATE LIBRARY & ARCHIVES COMMISSION*

During the Civil War, Houston often drove through Texas in his black buggy. One day after martial law was declared he was stopped by a sentry who demanded to see his pass. "Go to San Jacinto and learn my right to travel in Texas," Houston growled as he snapped the reins and passed the sentry.

Sam Houston died in bed on July 26, 1863. His last words to his wife were, "Texas, Margaret, Texas."

settlers to Nacogdoches; they had oxen, and these would slow them down for many days. Santa Anna had plenty of time. He sent word that General Cós should prepare to join him with 500 men; that would assure his superiority over the ragtag Army of Texas.

On April 18, Santa Anna burned Harrisburg and set out for New Washington. He wanted to see if Almonte had succeeded in intercepting the Texas government. He discovered that they had missed the government by a hair; when the dragoons arrived the cabinet was in a boat, pulling for a ship off-shore. The boat was within rifle range, but there was a woman, Mrs. Burnet, in it. Almonte told the dragoons to hold their fire. Because of his chivalry, the cabinet made its escape. Santa Anna had at least separated the Texas government from the Texas Army. Now all he had to do was deal with that army. To do so, he decided to seize Lynchburg and cut the Army off from further retreat. On the morning of April 19, he set out.

The April rains continued, turning the Brazos bottomland into one gigantic swamp, but the Texas Army swept on. Two days after the crossing of the Brazos, the hour of decision arrived at a fork in the road known as the Which Way Tree. To the left lay Nacogdoches and safety. To the right, Lynchburg, Harrisburg, and Santa Anna's army. Houston arrived at the Which Way Tree and turned to the right. A great cheer rose up in the ranks. At long last they were going into battle.

The army had to pause at the Which Way Tree; the colonists were separating here. Houston had agreed to send a hundred men along to Nacogdoches with them but there was no need; two hundred men deserted here rather than go into battle. The Texas Army was now at rock bottom; there were fewer than 1,000 men. However, all the layabouts had disappeared, and what was left was a hard-core group of fighters. Here also they lost some of their precious oxen; Mrs. Pamela Mann had lent the army four oxen when they left Groce's, and she wanted them back. When Houston said she could not have them, she stepped up, cut the traces, and led them off on the road to Nacogdoches amid cheers.

General Houston increased the pace of the march. In just three days from Groce's they reached the north bank of Buffalo Bayou, opposite the ruins of Harrisburg. They arrived on the night of April 18 to learn from a captured Mexican courier that Santa Anna was marching towards Lynchburg, and that another unit was coming to join him; meanwhile, the main body of the army under General Filisola awaited orders.

That evening, Houston made his only speech of the campaign. He assembled the men around him, raised his voice, and said, "Some of you may be killed, but soldiers, Remember the Alamo!"

He had touched a nerve. The soldiers took up the cry: "Remember the Alamo! Remember Goliad!"

After that, General Houston called in Juan Seguín. He was worried about the Tejanos in the army. Since Goliad the Texians had become violently anti-Mexican, and the Tejanos looked like Mexicans. The captain and his men might get killed by their friends on the battlefield. The general ordered them to stay behind and guard the baggage.

The captain bridled: "You must remember, General, that all my men are not with me tonight. Some of them fell at the Alamo. Besides, all of my men are from Béxar. Until Santa Anna and his army are driven out of Texas we cannot return home. We have more reason to kill Santanista than anyone else. We insist on coming."

General Houston smiled then, and it was arranged that the Tejanos would wear pieces of cardboard in their hats to signify that they were part of the Texas Army.

Now Houston had to move swiftly. He knew that Santa Anna was marching. He had to get to Lynch's Ferry first.

FOURTEEN

❧

The Battle of San Jacinto

The morale of the men of the Texas Army could not have been higher that day as they marched towards battle. Their general had committed himself at last, and they were going to fight. As they passed the ruins of Harrisburg they had shuddered; "Look," they said, "The Mexicans did that, too," and in their minds Harrisburg was added to the crimes for which they sought vengeance.

Early on the morning of April 19, they crossed Buffalo Bayou by log raft and leaky boat. Since the crossing took several hours, General Houston waited on the south bank and wrote a letter to his friend Henry Raguet at Nacogdoches:

> This morning we are preparing to meet Santa Anna. It is the only chance of saving Texas. From time to time I have looked for reinforcements in vain. The Convention adjourning to Harrisburg struck *panic* throughout the country. Texas could have started at least 4000 men. We will only have about seven hundred to march with besides the camp guard. We go to conquer.

The crossing completed, the Texas Army left a camp guard with the baggage and the sick. They set out for Lynch's Ferry, which was the key to the defense that Houston had planned on the field at San Jacinto. This triangular field was bounded on three sides by water and marsh, and was accessible only by that ferry which connected the northern apex of the triangle with Lynchburg, the hamlet on the San Jacinto River. If Santa Anna got to the ferry first, he could cross and take possession of the high ground.

They marched for two hours, then the general called a halt for breakfast. The hungry men gathered firewood and built campfires while the butchers did their work, and soon steaks were sizzling on the fires. Then a scout came riding in with a message: Santa Anna had burned New Washington and was marching toward Lynch's Ferry.

The men jumped up from their campfires. The lucky few grabbed a steak as they ran for their weapons and their mounts. In five minutes they were on the march again through the flooded countryside, where the wagons bogged down at every rivulet and had to be unloaded, and the goods carried across and loaded again at the other side. But there was a difference: grim smiles and no complaints now. They were going into battle.

The Texas Army marched all that day and all that night.

As the sun came up on the morning of April 20, they reached the San Jacinto plain, which spread across the northern tip of a peninsula that was virtually an island. Buffalo Bayou was on one side, 300 feet wide and 30 feet deep at spots. On the other side ran the San Jacinto River, and near the bottom of the dry land was a shallow mudhole known as Peggy Lake. Beyond that was marshland.

General Houston marched them to the stand of live oak, magnolias, hyacinths, and rhododendrons at the top of the peninsula. Spanish moss dripped from the trees. Here on the bayou side they made their camp, with the wagons and Colonel Neill's artillery in the trees. The ground sloped downward, rose again in 200 yards, and then sloped down again to Peggy Lake and beyond that, the swamp and the river. Earlier, Houston had spoken of meeting Santa Anna on "my own ground," and this was where he meant. The Guadalupe River country was Santa Anna country, eminently suited for cavalry charges and massed infantry maneuvers; there the Mexicans had the definite advantage. But this terrain was like that of the Mississippi and Louisiana forests, plenty of trees for a rifleman to hide behind, plenty of brush to conceal his movements, and too much moisture for a cavalry charge.

Having made camp on the high ground, the next order of business was food.

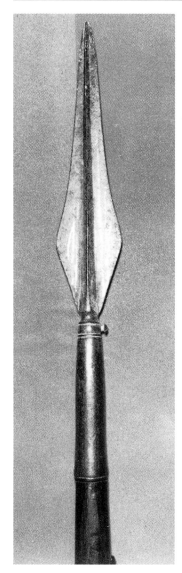

The butchers got busy again, the campfires were built, and the men feasted without interruption.

Three hours later Santa Anna arrived with his 650 men of the mobile unit. They had satisfied Santa Anna's curiosity with the dash to New Washington. The Texas government had escaped, and the excursion had cost them first position on the field of battle, but Santa Anna was still supremely confident of victory; he had reinforcements coming the next day and he knew that the Texas government's connection with the Texas army had been broken. If the general could win the day, the rebellion would be finished.

Santa Anna gave the order to pitch camp. He chose the land between Peggy Lake and the river, the only solid ground available to him. On his right was a grove of live oak behind a nameless mudhole with a brook that ran to Peggy Lake.

The Matamoros battalion was chosen for the front position, behind the breastworks. The cannon was placed in the trees to the right, with five companies of *cazadores* (light infantry) on the right flank and five companies of *granaderos* (grenadiers) on the left, with Santa Anna's personal guard of lancers behind them. These dispositions took Santa Anna's entire force of 650 men and there were no reserves. Santa Anna's silk tent was pitched behind the Matamoros; his the staff was in back, next to Peggy Lake.

Colonel Delgado, the artillery officer, took one look at the site and shuddered. Any youngster could have done better in choosing a site, he said. What ground did the Mexicans have for retreating in case of catastrophe? He answered his own question: none. Then he cornered General Castrillón with the question. The general could only sympathize; Santa Anna's arbitrary nature was well known.

Santa Anna could not see the enemy, so darkly was he shrouded in the rain forest, so he ordered a probe. A skirmish line of infantry set out across no-man's-land under the eye of the twelve-pound cannon known as the Golden Standard or *El Volcán*. The Mexican cannon spewed forth grapeshot, a ball of which caught Colonel Neill in the thigh. The Twin Sisters replied, damaging the Golden Standard's carriage, and the Mexicans retreated to their lines, where their comrades were building a barricade of packing boxes and brush. Seeing the Mexicans retreating without their gun, the Texas men raised a cheer.

The rest of the afternoon was quiet, save for occasional rifle fire from both sides. Seeing the Golden Standard abandoned on the field, Col. Sidney Sherman, commander of the Texas cavalry, asked permission to try to capture the gun. Permission was refused by General Houston, who knew and respected the superior strength of the Mexican lancers. Late in the afternoon, Sherman asked to make a cavalry reconnaissance into the field. Houston acceded, warning, however, that the Texas cavalry were to make no move toward the gun. Shortly before sunset, the Texas mounted riflemen set out, led by Colonel Sherman. One account says there were fifty-two mounted men, another reports more than eighty; the accounts agree that Secretary of War Thomas Jefferson Rusk was among them.

The Mexican cavalry rode forth to rescue the Golden Standard. Sherman could not resist the temptation; as soon as he saw the enemy, he ordered a charge. The mounted riflemen fired, but as soon as they fired they had to dismount to reload, and as they dismounted, the Mexican cavalry charged in with lowered lances. Enough of the riflemen had reloaded to fire a volley, and the Mexicans wheeled, fell back, regrouped, and came in again. The riflemen loaded again, but this time the lancers were too quick for them and a wild fight ensued, clubbed rifle and bowie knife against sabre and lance.

MIRABEAU BUONAPARTE LAMAR, WHO TOOK PART IN THE BATTLE OF SAN JACINTO. LATER, HE SERVED AS SECOND PRESIDENT OF THE REPUBLIC OF TEXAS, FOLLOWING SAM HOUSTON'S TERM. *TEXAS STATE LIBRARY & ARCHIVES COMMISSION*

Secretary Rusk was surrounded, and would have been captured or killed save for the quick action of Pvt. Mirabeau Buonaparte Lamar, who spurred his big stallion into the fray, knocked aside a Mexican pony, and cleared the path for Rusk to escape. Meanwhile, the Mexican cavalry rescued the twelve-pounder and got it back inside the Mexican lines.

Seeing the Texas cavalry in trouble, Capt. Jesse Billingsley ordered his company of infantry into action. As they passed by General Houston, he ordered them back into line and they laughed at him.

"Countermarch back to the safety of the timber!" Houston repeated.

Erastus "Deaf" Smith
1787–1837

Deaf Smith was Gen. Sam Houston's most valued scout. He saved the tiny Texas Army by keeping track of the movements of the three Mexican columns that were advancing on them as the general led a strategic retreat in 1836 deep into the Brazos River bottomland.

Smith gained his frontiersman's skills in Mississippi before he settled in San Antonio in 1821 and married Guadelupe Ruiz de Durán. The couple had several children; Smith's descendants still live in Texas.

His deafness began in childhood and increased with age, so that by the time he met General Houston he could carry on conversations only by lipreading. Smith joined the revolutionary army at the beginning, and with his son-in-law, a free black man named Hendrick Arnold, Deaf Smith led Ben Milam's volunteers through the streets of San Antonio in the attack that captured that city. On the eve of the Battle of San Jacinto he destroyed Vince's Bridge, a connecting link to the battlefield that crossed a small bayou, thus inhibiting the line of retreat of both sides from the battlefield.

Smith's last service to Texas was on February 17, 1837, when he commanded a band of Texas Rangers that intercepted a Mexican incursion into Laredo. When he died and his friends learned that he had left no money, they secured from the struggling Republic of Texas government a $500-per-year pension for his widow.

A PORTRAIT OF ERASTUS "DEAF" SMITH, FAMOUS SCOUT AND RANGING COMPANY LEADER OF COLONIAL TEXAS AND THE TEXAS REVOLUTION, IS DEPICTED ON THE RIGHT-HAND SIDE OF THIS REPUBLIC OF TEXAS FIVE-DOLLAR NOTE.
EUGENE C. BARKER LIBRARY, CENTER FOR AMERICAN HISTORY, UNIVERSITY OF TEXAS AT AUSTIN

"Countermarch yourself!" shouted a soldier as they passed him. In a moment, every company was moving and Colonel Burleson was leading the charge. They drove the enemy back behind his breastworks and Colonel Sherman called his horsemen to retreat to the Texas woods. But an inexperienced rider, Walter Lane, got into trouble. A Mexican lancer speared him in the shoulder and knocked him off his horse. He fell like a dead man, but in a moment he was up, and staggering toward the Texas line. He was surrounded by

Manuel Fernandez Castrillón
?=1836

Manuel Fernandez Castrillón was born in Havana, Cuba. He joined the Imperial Spanish Army and worked his way through the ranks, participating in dozens of battles. Coming to Mexico with the Spanish army, he changed sides during the revolution and joined the republicans.

Castrillón was well educated and intelligent. By the beginning of the Texas campaign, he had become a brigadier general and served as Santa Anna's aide-de-camp. He wasn't afraid of Santa Anna's wrath, and he opposed the March 6, 1836, assault on the Alamo, wishing to wait until the heavy cannon arrived. He knew his general very well, and understood that Santa Anna was capricious, opinionated, stubborn, and often stupid—he even said this to Colonel Delgado within Santa Anna's hearing.

During the attack on the Alamo, Castrillón rallied the troops of two battalions after their commanders had fallen and led the combined force to the north wall. He tried in vain to save the lives of six prisoners who surrendered, believing one of them was Davy Crockett, but was rebuffed by Santa Anna, who insisted on their execution.

Later, in the battle of San Jacinto, the Texian attack surprised Castrillón while he was making his morning toilet. He dropped his razor, picked up his sword, and went out of his tent to rally the troops. They implored him to flee but he refused, folding his arms and waiting for death. It was not long in coming, although Secretary Rusk tried to save Castrillón's life and knocked aside several rifle barrels that were aimed at the general. In the end, however, the vengeful Texians shot him down.

Mexican lancers ready to spear him again when Lamar rode up, drew his pistol, shot one lancer, and charged another. Henry Karnes rode up, pulled Lane up behind him, and sped off to safety. The Mexican cavalrymen, ever mindful of an act of valor, cheered. Lamar stopped, turned, and bowed to them in acknowledgment, and the Texians cheered.

But General Houston was angry with his troops. Colonel Sherman had disobeyed orders. Two men had been wounded and several horses lost. The entire infantry regiment had disobeyed orders, although there had been no casualties. The general congratulated Colonel Sherman on his valor but demoted him by putting him in charge of a company of riflemen. Pvt. Mirabeau Lamar was advanced to colonel's rank and given the cavalry. Houston could hardly discipline an entire regiment while in battle.

The Mexicans withdrew to the position in front of Peggy Lake and began to fortify it as best they could. The Golden Standard was placed in the middle of the line, with breastworks on both sides. The breastworks were strengthened with saddles, sacks of beans, and brush. The Mexican soldiers labored on their five-foot-high fortifications all afternoon and late into the night.

The soldiers of the Texas Army gathered around their campfires that night and talked about attacking. Houston retired to his tent under a big oak tree and read from Julius Caesar's *Gallic Wars* half the night and planned the Texas attack for the following day. He also gave orders that he was not to be disturbed; he had slept an average of three hours a night for the previous two weeks.

At dawn on the morning of April 21 the Mexicans expected an attack. None came.

The Texians sat around their fires, grousing about their general, sharpening their knives, and cleaning their firearms. The mounted men groomed their horses and oiled their saddles. At nine o'clock, General Cós arrived at the Mexican camp with 540 men and a pack train of mules; they had marched all night and crossed Vince's Bridge at Lynch's Ferry. Santa Anna was furious with his brother-in-law because most of the new soldiers were recruits, but his army now outnumbered the Texas Army and somewhere nearby was General Filisola with the main body.

The new arrivals were exhausted from their long march but they had to make camp; the Preferencia company took the extreme right, butting up against the trees, and the Aldama battalion rested on the left. Then the newcomers stacked arms, put up their tents, and lay down to rest. Santa Anna and his men were exhausted from their long night of effort on the redoubt, so they did the same. General Santa Anna didn't even put out pickets to warn the camp of impending attack. The horses were unsaddled and put out to graze down by the river.

The Texians observed the coming of the reinforcements with various degrees of dismay. "A hot time is preparing for us—the enemy is increasing," said Deaf Smith, who suggested that he might take some men and destroy Vince's Bridge, so that no more Mexicans could come.

General Houston told him to reconnoiter first to see how many men Santa Anna had. So Smith picked up Walter Lane and they mounted their horses, rode around the Mexican camp, and stopped about 300 yards behind it. Lane held the scout's horse while he dismounted and took out his telescope to begin counting tents. He was spotted from the camp, and soon bullets were whizzing about their ears. Smith paid no heed, but went on with his count until a troop of Mexican cavalry came after them.

"Lane," he said, "I think these fellers are a-shootin' at us. Let's git!"

He climbed on his horse again and the pair rode back to the Texas camp. Deaf Smith reported his findings; General Houston told him to go ahead and destroy Vince's Bridge. Smith rounded up half a dozen riders and they set out on the five-mile ride to the bridge.

At about noon, the officers and men began to grow visibly upset about the delay in attacking. The officers demanded a council and General Houston acceded, although that wasn't his style. The officers assembled and everyone had his say. They argued back and forth: Should they attack or should they wait in their superb defense position for the Mexicans to attack? General Houston took no position but let them argue. Finally they came to an impasse, and he dismissed the council with the observation that perhaps they ought to wait until the next day to attack. The dismay of the men was such that mutiny seemed to threaten.

It was then that the general told the men to get their dinners, then he would lead them into battle.

At 3:30 in the afternoon, while the Mexican camp still slept, General Houston mounted his white horse, Saracen. Then he formed his army into battle array. They set out across no-man's-land in three columns with the Twin Sisters, then deployed into a long line that extended across the field, two men deep. Every soldier carried a rifle or a musket with bayonet—after the fight at the Alamo, bayonets were standard issue—and every man had a sword or a bowie knife and two or three pistols stuck in his belt. The Twin Sisters were in the middle of the line; General Houston, on his white stallion, was in the center. Sword in hand, he waved the army forward. The color bearer of the 2nd

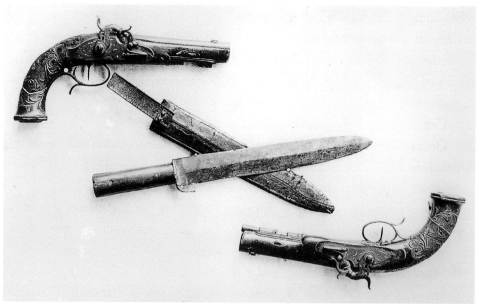

BOWIE KNIFE AND PISTOLS BELONGING TO PETER H. BELL.
TEXAS STATE LIBRARY & ARCHIVES COMMISSION

Texian Regiment unfurled the banner, a bare-breasted Liberty bearing a sabre from which dangled a ribbon inscribed "Liberty or death."

The men had been told to hold their fire, and for once they obeyed the order to the letter. They were urged onward by a German fifer and a black drummer, whose only common air was an old favorite, "Will You Come to the Bower?" They played this song time after time as General Houston's stallion pranced along the line.

In the Mexican camp a bugler of the Matamoros battalion sounded the alarm, and his fellows fired their muskets. The Golden Standard spewed a load of grapeshot at the Texas line. But in their hurry, the infantry fired high.

General Castrillón was shaving in his tent. He dropped his razor, picked up his sword, and ran out of the tent shouting orders.

But it was already too late; the Texians were on them. When Houston's army reached the edge of the rise in the middle of no-man's-land, the Twin Sisters were swung around into firing position and began to sing. They were loaded with chopped horseshoes, and this improvised grapeshot tore through the Mexican ranks.

The riflemen rushed the Mexican breastworks, firing; there was no trace of the gentle warriors of the assault on San Antonio just five months earlier, no dis-arming and paroling. These were demons filled with blood lust. One Mexican officer attributed the ferocity to corn whiskey, but today no whiskey was needed.

Colonel Delgado stood up on an empty ammunition crate behind the breastworks to survey the scene. He saw General Castrillón on one side, shouting orders, Colonel Almonte on the other side, shouting orders. No one was listening. General Santa Anna emerged from his tent and he shouted at the men: "Lie down! You will be hit!"

Other officers yelled, "Commence firing!"

On the Texas side, after the first volley General Houston tried to get the riflemen to reload, but Secretary Rusk rode up.

"If we stop we are cut to pieces—don't stop—Give them hell!"

The Texas Army surged forward over the breastworks, shouting, "Remember The Alamo!" Their rifles became clubs, and bowie knives and pistols came out.

"Remember Goliad!" they cried.

Frantically, the Mexican gunners worked the Golden Standard. They fired five times, and grapeshot and mine balls thinned the Texas ranks, but then the gunners were overwhelmed.

A few of the Mexican musketeers and riflemen rushed to the breastworks

THE FEROCIOUS COMBAT LASTED ONLY EIGHTEEN MINUTES AS THE TEXAS ARMY VENTED ITS RAGE ON SANTA ANNA'S TROOPS. FOLLOWING THE MERCILESS ATTACK ON THE ALAMO AND THE GOLIAD MASSACRE, EACH MAN FOUGHT NOT ONLY FOR TEXAS, BUT FOR FALLEN FAMILY AND FRIENDS. HENRY A. MCARDLE'S 1895 PAINTING, THE BATTLE OF SAN JACINTO, DETAILS THE INTENSITY OF THE CONFLICT.
TEXAS STATE LIBRARY & ARCHIVES COMMISSION

and snapped off shots. They were aiming at General Houston and five bullets struck Saracen, felling him. Houston mounted another horse, but that one too fell before the musket fire. A shot struck Houston in the Achilles tendon of his right foot, breaking his ankle. He flung himself onto a third horse and remained on the field.

The 2nd Texas Regiment drove into the front of the Matamoros battalion. Seconds later, the 1st Texas came up on the right; the two regiments overran the gun and took the breastworks and the left-hand copse of woods. Lamar's cavalry overwhelmed the *grenaderos*.

Eight miles away, Texas baggage guards had Captain Bachillar, a special courier for Santa Anna captured the day before by Deaf Smith, tied to a tree. All of them were following the action. First came the deep bellow of the Golden Standard, then the popping of the Twin Sisters, and then the rattle of small arms.

In the beginning moments the captain was quite lively, but then he sank into silence.

"Santa Anna is whipped," he said at last.

"How do you know that?"

"Because I don't hear the sound of his guns."

Remember the Alamo!

Jimmie Curtis had special reason to remember: his son-in-law, George Washington Cottle, had fallen at the Alamo, and so had his brother-in-law, Thomas J. Jackson. Curtis clubbed his rifle and went tearing through the gap in the breastworks, lambasting and breaking skulls to right and left.

"You killed Wash Cottle," he thundered. "Remember The Alamo! You killed Tom Jackson. Remember The Alamo!"

Col. John Wharton tried to stop the slaughter. He saw Jimmie Curtis threatening a Mexican officer with a bowie knife. "You killed Wash Cottle," he said. "Now I'm going to kill you and make a razorstrop of your hide."

The colonel hoisted the Mexican officer up behind him on his horse. "Men, this Mexican is mine," Wharton said.

Jimmie Curtis took aim and blasted the Mexican off the back of the horse, turned and walked away.

Other soldiers had lost relatives in the Goliad Massacre and they now got back some of their own, slashing, bashing, and shooting every Mexican they encountered.

Remember Goliad!

Colonel Delgado observed General Santa Anna. "I saw His Excellency

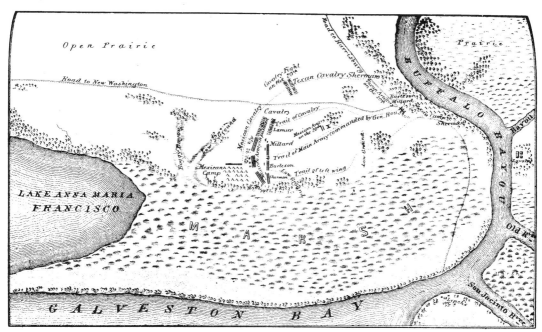

THIS MAP OF THE SAN JACINTO BATTLEGROUND DESCRIBES THE POSITIONS OF
THE OPPOSING ARMIES AND THE ROUTES OF THE FORCES AS THEY MET IN COM-
BAT. IT APPEARS IN *HISTORY OF TEXAS* BY HENDERSON YOAKUM.

running about in the utmost excitement, wringing his hands, unable to give an
order."

General Castrillón was on the ground with a leg wound. Colonel Trevino
was killed, and Colonel Aguirre sorely wounded.

Colonel Delgado tried to rally the men, but they were beyond recall; discipline had broken completely and they had become a senseless mob "flying in
small groups, terrified, and sheltering behind large trees...all efforts were in vain,
the evil was beyond remedy: they were a bewildered and panic-stricken herd."

Delgado tried to mount his horse, but the confusion had panicked the beast
and he would not stand still. Delgado left the field, leading his horse. He saw
General Santa Anna ride by; the commander had commandeered a horse from
one of his officers and was fleeing from the battlefield.

Delgado's last view of General Castrillón was a heroic one; the general had
recovered enough to mount an ammunition case, and arms folded, was glaring
down at his enemies. His men called him to flee with them, but he refused. "I
have been in forty battles," he said, "and I have never yet turned my back on the
enemy. I am too old to change."

Secretary Rusk tried to save the old general. "Don't shoot!" he yelled to the
other Texians. "Don't shoot!" He threw up several rifle barrels that were aiming

U.S. PISTOL.

MEXICAN CAVALRY PISTOL.

U.S. PISTOL.

WEST POINT MUSEUM COLLECTIONS, UNITED STATES MILITARY ACADEMY

MEXICAN BROWN BESS MUSKET.

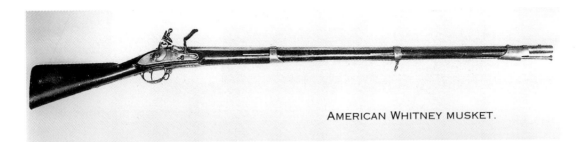

AMERICAN WHITNEY MUSKET.

MEXICAN CARBINE.

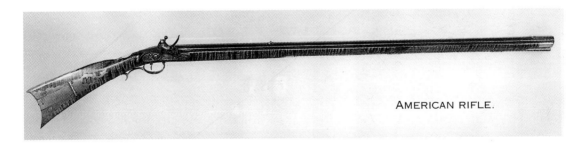

AMERICAN RIFLE.

U.S. MILITIA ARTILLERY OFFICER'S SWORD.

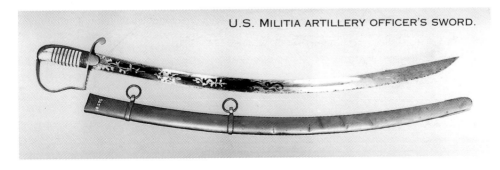

WEST POINT MUSEUM COLLECTIONS, UNITED STATES MILITARY ACADEMY

at the general. But other Texians drew a bead on the general's chest and riddled him with bullets.

Colonel Wharton tried again. They had done enough killing. He rode along the shore of Peggy Lake, where the Mexicans were floundering in the water and being mercilessly executed.

"Me no Alamo. Me no Goliad," one boy cried to a soldier on the bank. The Texian soldier took aim with his musket and shot the boy in the head.

Wharton ordered his men to cease fire.

J. H. T. Dixon, one of the executioners, replied. "Colonel, if Jesus Christ were to come down from Heaven and order me to quit shooting Santanistas I wouldn't do it, sir." And he stepped back, cocked his rifle, and pointed it at the colonel's chest. Colonel Wharton reined his horse and rode away.

General Houston could do no better. He ordered his drummer to beat retreat, and when that did not produce anything he lifted his voice and bellowed, "Parade, men. Parade." No one was listening. Houston then shouted in exasperation. "Gentlemen, gentlemen, gentlemen!"

Momentary silence descended.

"I applaud your bravery," he said, "but damn your manners."

Then he rode off the field, leaving the men to their orgy of slaughter.

The battle lasted only eighteen minutes, but the slaughter continued all afternoon. One brave captain summarized the attitude: "You know how to take prisoners: Take them with the butt of your gun, club guns and

Remember The Alamo!

Remember Goliad!

Club guns, right and left and nock [sic] their brains out!"

On the right of the Mexican camp, about a hundred yards from the tents, was a small grove of trees and a mudhole with a stream leading to Peggy Lake. The Mexicans fled the camp, heading for the grove and for Peggy Lake. Here the greatest carnage occurred.

Having reached the lake, Colonel Almonte swam with one hand and held his sabre above his head with the other, urging his men to follow. At the lake and across the field Mexicans fell to their knees, asking clemency.

"Me no Alamo. Me no Goliad," they said, clutching at their executioners, begging to surrender, begging for mercy. But there was no mercy this day.

Stephen Austin's cousin, Sgt. Moses Bryan, encountered a young Mexican drummer boy lying on his face, both legs broken. One of the Texas soldiers pricked him with the point of a bayonet. The boy grabbed his legs and cried.

"Ave Maria purissima. Por Dios salva mi vida!"

Sergeant Bryan begged the soldier to spare the boy. "The man looked at me and put his hand on his pistol," Bryan recalled. "I moved away and just as I did so, he blew out the boy's brains."

Scores of Mexicans rushed to the lake and jumped in, jammed all together. Seeing the jam-up, the Texians positioned themselves on the bank. It was like shooting fish in a barrel.

Pvt. William Foster Young recalled, "I sat there on the shore and shot them until my ammunition ran out, then I turned the butt of my musket and began knocking them in the head."

Juan Seguín's Tejanos were in the thick of it, shouting, *"Recuerda el Alamo!"*

A Mexican officer recognized Tejano soldier Antonio Menchaca as an acquaintance and pleaded with him as a brother Mexican to intercede for his life.

Menchaca looked at him coldly. "No, damn you," he said, "I'm not Mexican. I'm an American," and turning to his Texian comrades, he said, "Shoot him!"

In the end, Colonel Almonte managed to round up 400 Mexicans to surrender to Secretary Rusk, who took personal charge of them and brought them to safety. In all there were 730 prisoners, 200 of them wounded, and 630 bodies. The Texas Army lost nine men. The Mexican death toll in this Battle of San Jacinto was higher than that of Texas in all the previous engagements of the war. General Houston had pursued his strategy, he had chosen the time and place to fight, and he had won.

FIFTEEN

❧

Independence

In spite of his wound, General Houston had remained in the saddle all during the battle and well after the senseless killing began. He finally felt weak from loss of blood and rode back across the field, accepting the cheers of his men and waving. He reached the oak tree where he had slept the night before, tried to dismount, and collapsed. His men got him onto a blanket underneath the tree and called the surgeon.

Immediately after the battle, Houston wondered what had become of General Santa Anna. His officers reported that the Mexican commander had taken one of their horses and dashed off the field; that was all they knew. Texas horsemen had chased him as far as the remains of Vince's Bridge but had lost him there. Actually, he had fallen off his horse and the horse had run away. He had waded across the bayou in chest-high water, then hid for several hours in a thicket of pines. After that he had made his way to a deserted house, where he found some clothing and changed to disguise himself. Santa Anna spent a lonely, miserable, and hungry night in the deserted house.

On the day after the battle, a party searching for Mexican prisoners picked him up but did not recognize in this ragged figure in faded white linen trousers and an old trooper's jacket the supreme commander of the Mexican army. He was interrogated but unrecognized, although he wore a diamond stud in his shirt. He said he was just a cavalry trooper. The Texas soldiers told him they

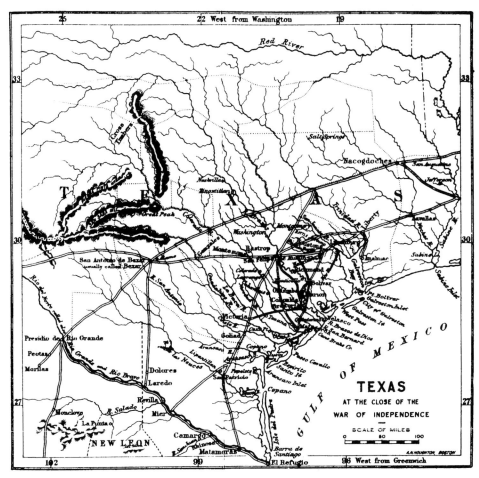

A MAP OF TEXAS AT THE CLOSE OF THE WAR OF INDEPENDENCE, 1836.
UT INSTITUTE OF TEXAN CULTURES AT SAN ANTONIO

were looking for General Santa Anna and asked if he knew where he was. He said he had heard that Santa Anna had escaped via Thompson's Pass to the south. That actually was a true statement of Santa Anna's intent—he had been heading for General Filisola's main force.

Walking ahead of his mounted captors, and prodded from time to time by the point of a lance, the prisoner stumbled two miles back toward the camp, but finally complained that he could go no farther; he had lost his slippers and his feet were bleeding. One of his captors suggested that they shoot him, but the other one took pity on him and gave him a hand up, so he rode into camp on the back of his captor's horse.

As they approached the Texas camp, the prisoner showed a lively interest in the battle of the day before. Was that General Houston who had led the

Vicente Filisola
1789–1850

Vicente Filisola was one of Mexico's most able generals in the first half of the nineteenth century. He was an Italian who at age fifteen emigrated to Spain and joined the Spanish Army, where he rose rapidly in rank. By 1810, he had been promoted to lieutenant with citations for bravery in action.

Filisola went to Mexico with General Iturbide's army and by 1821 had been promoted to lieutenant colonel to command 4,000 troops, the largest unit of the Spanish Army in Mexico. When Iturbide declared himself Emperor, Filisola was promoted to brigadier general and sent to Central America to annex the states there to the Mexican Empire. He had virtually accomplished that mission when the empire began to fall apart.

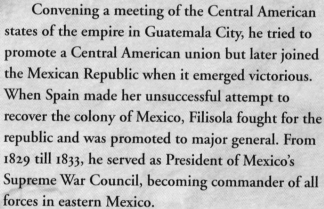

Convening a meeting of the Central American states of the empire in Guatemala City, he tried to promote a Central American union but later joined the Mexican Republic when it emerged victorious. When Spain made her unsuccessful attempt to recover the colony of Mexico, Filisola fought for the republic and was promoted to major general. From 1829 till 1833, he served as President of Mexico's Supreme War Council, becoming commander of all forces in eastern Mexico.

Ill health then forced him to retire, but it seems to have been a political illness. In 1835, Filisola was

GEN. VICENTE FILISOLA, SANTA ANNA'S SECOND-IN-COMMAND OF THE ARMY OF OPERATIONS IN THE TEXAS WAR. HE WAS MEXICO'S BEST ADMINISTRATIVE GENERAL. AFTER SANTA ANNA WAS CAPTURED AT THE BATTLE OF SAN JACINTO, FILISOLA FOLLOWED HIS ORDERS AND REMOVED THE MEXICAN ARMY FROM TEXAS SOIL. FOR THIS HE WAS LATER COURT-MARTIALED, FOR FAILING HIS DUTIES TO THE NATION, AND LATER ACQUITTED. PHOTO FROM *THE SECOND MEXICAN-TEXAS WAR* BY GEN. MIGUEL SANCHEZ LAMEGO.
HILL JR. COLLEGE, WACO, TEXAS

recalled to duty and became General Santa Anna's right-hand man during the Texas rebellion. After Santa Anna was captured at the Battle of San Jacinto, General Filisola loyally obeyed the orders to remove the Mexican army from Texas, an act for which he was later criticized and court-martialed. He was imprisoned for this in 1840 but was later cleared and restored to duty.

In the Mexican-American War, he commanded a division in Chihuahua. After the war he once again became president of the War Council, a post he held until he died of cholera in 1850. Filisola was Mexico's most competent administrative general in Santa Anna's day, honest and apolitical, but very dour in outlook. He was called "the least Italian of Italians." He had no personal ambitions and did not care for wealth, leaving only a modest estate.

Texians? he asked. What was to become of the prisoners? And how many Mexicans had been killed?

That question showed his attitude, a combination of imperiousness and supplication. It was answered partially as they approached the camp and saw the piles of bodies on the ground. As they came up to a band of prisoners, there were cries of "*El Presidente, El Presidente,*" and the secret was out. The patrol had captured Santa Anna.

Unmasked, Santa Anna requested an audience with General Houston. They took him to the oak tree beneath which the general was dozing, in some pain from his shattered ankle. Houston looked up as the captive sat down. A crowd gathered, waiting for the sentence of death. They had been looking for Santa Anna since dawn; they had even demanded a list of all the Mexican officers, thinking that he might have concealed himself among them. Now they had found him, and they wanted blood.

Colonel Almonte was summoned as interpreter and Santa Anna approached in a lordly manner. "I am General Antonio López de Santa Anna," he said, "President of Mexico and commander in chief of the Army of Operations. I put myself at the disposal of the brave General Houston. I wish to be treated as a general should be when a prisoner of war."

Houston lifted himself up on one elbow.

"Good afternoon," he said pleasantly. "Ah, Santa Anna. Ah, indeed. Take a seat, general. I'm glad to see you."

Santa Anna seated himself on a box. "That man may consider himself born

WOUNDED IN THE FOOT DURING THE BATTLE OF SAN JACINTO, GEN. SAM
HOUSTON SAT UNDER A TREE WHEN HE MET WITH SANTA ANNA TO ACCEPT HIS
SURRENDER. THE MEXICAN GENERAL CONGRATULATED HOUSTON ON DEFEATING
"THE NAPOLEON OF THE WEST." THIS VERSION OF THE SCENE IS WILLIAM HENRY
HUDDLE'S *THE SURRENDER OF SANTA ANNA*, PAINTED IN 1886.
TEXAS STATE LIBRARY & ARCHIVES COMMISSION

to no common destiny who has conquered the Napoleon of the West," he said.
"And now it remains for him to be generous with the vanquished."

"You should have remembered that at the Alamo," Houston said.

"What happened at the Alamo—I was only obeying the orders of my government," Santa Anna began.

Houston lost his temper. "You are the government of Mexico, sir," he said.
"A dictator has no superior. What about the murders at Goliad?"

"Those were the responsibility of General Urrea," Santa Anna lied. "And
when I have the opportunity I shall have him executed. He should never have
accepted the surrenders."

The crowd around the two men was growing restive; to a man they wanted
Santa Anna's head. General Houston, however, was wiser than the crowd. He
knew that General Urrea and General Filisola together had more than 3,500 soldiers on Texas soil and that under the more competent leadership of those two,
they might attack. He knew that he did not have the strength to fight another

battle, and he desperately wanted Texas to be free. Santa Anna wanted to stay alive; it was time to bargain.

Santa Anna offered to remove all the Mexican troops from Texas if he were freed to return to Mexico.

"It's not so simple as that," said General Houston. "I have no authority to negotiate a peace. That is for the civil government to do."

"Civil government, what is that? Surely the two parties who fought can arrive at an agreement."

"I'm sorry," said Houston. "I'm not empowered to negotiate. I can only offer you your life if you will order your troops across the Rio Grande."

Santa Anna looked around him at the Texians who stood, muttering, blood in their eyes. "All right," he said, "I will order General Filisola to leave Texas." He sat down then and wrote a letter:

> His excellency, Don Vicente Filisola, General of Division:
> Excellent Sir:
> Having yesterday with the small division under my immediate command, had an encounter with the enemy, which, notwithstanding I had previously observed all possible precautions, proved unfortunate. I am in consequence a prisoner of the enemy. Under these circumstances your excellency will order General Gaona, with his division, to countermarch to Béxar and wait for orders. Your Excellency will also, with the divisions under your command, march to the same place. The division under command of General Urrea will retire to Guadalupe Victoria. I have agreed with General Houston for an armistice until matters can be regulated so that the war will cease forever.

And with his customary flourish, he signed the letter. A Mexican express rider was sent to General Filisola with the orders.

Several hundred Texian families were concentrated at a camp near the ruins of Harrisburg, where they had been trapped by the convergence of Texan and Mexican military forces. At about six o'clock that evening, they saw a woman clap her hands and shout, "Hallelujah! Hallelujah!" The people around her thought she was mad, but following her gestures, they saw a man they knew riding hellbent for the camp, his horse's flanks flecked with foam. He was waving his hat and shouting, "San Jacinto! San Jacinto! The Mexicans are whipped and Santa Anna is a prisoner!"

People laughed and embraced and prayed and wept. As the night fell over the prairie and the moon rose above the forest of flowers, the soft southern wind brought with it the scent of peace. Texas was free.

On Galveston Island a few days later, President David Burnet and his cabinet read General Houston's official report of the Battle of San Jacinto. The president was noncommittal. He was not pleased, but nothing General Houston did seemed to please him. He began making arrangements to go to San Jacinto.

General Filisola proceeded to carry out General Santa Anna's orders, although General Urrea and others advised that he not pay any attention to Santa Anna's instructions because they were issued under duress. But Filisola knew the Mexican army was beaten—not by General Houston, but by the weather and climate and logistics. Filisola's supply line was extended to the breaking point and his men were suffering from dysentery and starvation. He would have found it impossible to make a forced march in this weather; he found it difficult enough to hold the army together to bring the men safely across the Rio Grande.

The President of Texas and his cabinet arrived at San Jacinto by steamer on May 4 to find that General Houston had moved the Texas Army camp three miles up the bayou to escape the stink of the rotting Mexican corpses. President Burnet was in his usual foul temper, and accused Houston of bad faith in not chasing General Filisola—quite disregarding the fact that Filisola's army outnumbered the Texas Army by four to one. What Burnet was really angry about was the division of spoils; Houston's officers had found $12,000 in silver in Santa Anna's luggage. Various officers inspected the loot, which brought the sum down to $7,000, and this was parceled out to the soldiers, giving each man about $12. Houston appropriated Santa Anna's ornate saddle, which he later gave away.

The news of the victory traveled as fast as a horse could run; it reached New Orleans and sent ships sailing for Texas bearing arms that were no longer needed. The Texians had not received any help from the American government and very little from Americans, but suddenly everyone wanted to share in the victory. Gen. Edmund Pendleton Gaines, commander of the neutral U.S. Army troops stationed in Texas on the Sabine River, sent a messenger to the White House and gave the word to President Andrew Jackson, who wrote Houston warning against killing Santa Anna, something Houston had no thought of doing. President Burnett and his assistant negotiated two treaties with Santa Anna, the public Treaty of Velasco and a secret treaty which freed Santa Anna to return to Mexico.

On May 9, the Texas Presidential party returned to Galveston on the *Yellow*

PAGE ONE OF THE PASSPORT OF GENERAL SANTA ANNA, WRITTEN BY GEN. SAM HOUSTON OF THE REPUBLIC OF TEXAS. TEXAS STATE LIBRARY & ARCHIVES COMMISSION

Stone. President Burnet tried to insist that Houston stay in San Jacinto with his army, but the general's wound was troubling him and he needed expert medical attention that he could not get in the field. Captain Ross of the *Yellow Stone* insisted that Houston be taken aboard, saying he would not sail without him, and Burnet had to yield. Houston was carried onto the ship by Secretary Rusk and his brother.

General Houston said goodbye to the Army of Texas. "When Liberty is established," he said, "it will be enough to say, 'I was a member of the Army of San Jacinto.'"

When they reached Galveston Island, the vindictive Burnet again denied Houston passage in the ship the politicians were taking to New Orleans. This time he was successful. Houston secured accommodations on the sailing schooner *Flora,* and arrived in New Orleans on May 22. It had been a month

SAM HOUSTON—THE RAVEN. OIL PORTRAIT BY WILLIAM HENRY HUDDLE.
TEXAS STATE LIBRARY & ARCHIVES COMMISSION

since the Battle of San Jacinto and word had spread across the United States. A huge crowd was on hand to welcome General Houston. He was very weak from his wound, but he managed to stand up and accept the admiration of the crowd at the dock, after which he fainted in the arms of his friends. He was taken to a private house where the doctors removed twenty splinters of bone from his ankle.

While Houston was in New Orleans, the Army of Texas was disintegrating.

President Burnet, in a typical caustic action, appointed Mirabeau Lamar as General of the Army but the soldiers would not accept Lamar as commander in chief. Under the provisions of the secret treaty, General Santa Anna was to be returned to Mexico intact. On May 14 he boarded the Texas Navy's ship *Invincible* for the return home, but the vessel had to wait for a favorable wind; while they were waiting, a ship carrying a hundred volunteers for the Texas

STEPHEN F. AUSTIN AS COMMISSIONER OF THE REPUBLIC OF TEXAS IN 1836. THIS PORTRAIT WAS EXECUTED ORIGINALLY IN NEW ORLEANS IN 1836 BY AN UNKNOWN ARTIST BUT COPIED IN 1873 BY LOUIS EYTH. THE ORIGINAL PORTRAIT HANGS IN THE STATE CAPITOL IN AUSTIN.
TEXAS STATE LIBRARY & ARCHIVES COMMISSION

Army pulled into Galveston. They had come to Texas in search of war, and now there was none. There was the relic of the war, the defeated Santa Anna, waiting for the wind to change. These filibusters (for that is what they were) demanded Santa Anna. President Burnet had him taken off, as they demanded, but landed him across the Brazos River at Quintana, where the mob could not get at him, and placed a troop of guards around Santa Anna and his entourage.

However, it was soon apparent that if Santa Anna was to survive he would have to be moved to a place of safety; there were four survivors of the Goliad Massacre in the mob.

Santa Anna was well aware of his danger. "The exaltation that [occured] because of my being brought ashore continued to increase to such an extent that every private felt himself called on to assassinate the Mexican President," he said later.

President Burnet ordered Santa Anna moved up the Brazos River to Columbia, but the problem remained. "The Butcher of the Alamo" was still under threat although he was moved again to the plantation of Dr. James Phelps, twelve miles north of Columbia. He was not sent back to Mexico, as the secret treaty provided.

Nor was the Treaty of Velasco honored; the Mexican government denounced it as having been made under duress and repudiated it. So a state of war continued to exist although Generals Filisola and Urrea took the Mexican army across the Rio Grande. Urrea objected, but Filisola was in command.

General Houston left New Orleans in the second week of June for Nacogdoches. His wound had still not healed, but he wanted to conceal that fact, so he did not skip public appearances.

He had two serious matters on his mind. One was the fate of General Santa Anna; thousands of Texians wanted him tried and sentenced to death for the killings at the Alamo and Goliad. But Houston knew, and his knowledge had been reinforced by Andrew Jackson, that to kill Santa Anna would be to write *finis* to Texas hopes of American annexation.

Besides this knotty problem, all summer he worried about the possibility of a new invasion of Texas by Mexico, which he called "the present crisis"; however, the crisis evaporated in the autumn without action. More serious was the crisis in Texas's government affairs. Most Texians wanted annexation to the United States, but before this could be achieved, Texas had to show that it had a stable government. In the summer of 1836 this was not true. President Burnet's government was inept and distrusted at home and abroad. Fortunately, David Burnet was sick of governing, and he scheduled elections for September 1836.

MIRABEAU BUONAPARTE LAMAR SERVED AS SAM HOUSTON'S VICE PRESIDENT OF THE REPUBLIC OF TEXAS. FOLLOWING HOUSTON'S TERM IN OFFICE, LAMAR BECAME THE REPUBLIC'S SECOND PRESIDENT.
TEXAS STATE LIBRARY & ARCHIVES COMMISSION

By law, Burnet could not succeed himself. The candidates were Stephen Austin, who was running only to further the cause of annexation to the United States; Henry Smith, the former provisional governor; and General Houston, who won the election by an overwhelming majority on September 5, 1836. Mirabeau Buonaparte Lamar was elected vice president. Other issues on the ballot were the acceptance of the Constitution of the Republic of Texas, and annexation by the United States. The Texas Constitution was approved, although the voters denied the Texas legislature the power to amend it. The annexation measure was approved overwhelmingly.

Texas now considered itself to be independent, although Mexico still maintained that it was part of a Mexican state. Texas had a fundamental law, and

President Houston appointed a cabinet of amity: Stephen Austin was Secretary of State and Henry Smith was Secretary of the Treasury.

The immediate problem was that there was no treasury; Texas was bankrupt and $500,000 in debt. Anarchy was in the air, the army had only a two-day supply of food for the troops, and two of the four ships of the Texas Navy were impounded in New York for failure to pay repair bills.

And in the background was the problem of General Santa Anna: He had been repudiated by the Mexican government, and Vice President Lamar was leading the pack baying for his execution. As if that were not enough, the Texas government didn't have the money to continue to support Santa Anna and his entourage.

President Houston went to the Texas Senate, which had the power to decide Santa Anna's fate, and pleaded his old enemy's case. It was vital to Texas that the general be released and sent to the United States, where he had an invitation from President Andrew Jackson. Houston won his point. The Texas Senate agreed that Santa Anna should be freed, and the general personally rode to the Phelps Plantation with a letter of introduction to President Andrew Jackson. On November 20, 1836, Santa Anna's party left with a special military

THE FIRST OFFICIAL FLAG OF THE REPUBLIC OF TEXAS, DESIGNED BY LORENZO DE ZAVALA. IT WAS BLUE WITH A SINGLE GOLD STAR, THE LETTERS T-E-X-A-S BETWEEN THE STAR'S POINTS. *UT INSTITUTE OF TEXAN CULTURES AT SAN ANTONIO*

Sam Houston as Politician

Even as a young man, Sam Houston knew where he wanted to go and how to get there. His early adult years were spent in the U.S. Army. When he went into politics in Tennessee and was elected to Congress, he continued his military career in the Tennessee militia. In October 1821, he was elected major general.

He was tall, good-looking, genial, and clever, and had a remarkable oratorical style. He modeled his career on that of Andrew Jackson. In Texas, Stephen Austin was chosen as general of the army that descended on San Antonio, and Houston was chosen as commander in chief, but without authority over this army. However, he successfully undermined Austin's authority, consulting with James Fannin, Judge Advocate General William Wharton, and James Bowie, who were his agents.

When Dr. James Grant and Frank Johnson stole a march on Houston and took over the Matamoros Expedition, Houston slyly made the long ride to Goliad from Gonzales and persuaded many of the troops to abandon the expedition and join Houston's force. Once, two of his lieutenants refused to accompany his army to Groce's Plantation from San Felipe, but rather than argue, Houston waited until they joined up later and then punished them. He kept his own counsel on the march from Groce's, and when the army reached the Which Way Tree and he turned to the right, into battle, he gained the immediate respect of the army. After the war was won, Houston affected not to want the presidency of the republic until the final hours of the campaign. Then he won overwhelmingly.

escort to protect them from assassination. They had a difficult journey, but arrived in Washington on January 7, 1837.

In the United States Santa Anna was wined and dined until Washington grew tired of him. Then he was sent back to Mexico on a battleship, to be greeted coolly by the government that had repudiated him. He retired to his estate and spent the next few weeks writing an *apologia* which blamed the military defeat at San Jacinto on General Filisola. Texas and America would hear from him again, but at least he had not been assassinated on Texas soil.

Texians continued to hope for American annexation until the winter of

1836. Then, seeing that no state had recognized the Lone Star Republic, President Jackson sent a message to the U.S. Congress, rejecting Texas's request for annexation. Texas would have to go it alone until 1845, when they were finally annexed by the United States.

The heroes of the Alamo were not forgotten; in the autumn of 1836 Lt. Col. Juan Seguín, as commander of the Texas Army post at San Antonio, ordered the disinterment of the ashes of the Alamo defenders, and buried them with dignity. He delivered a eulogy for his fallen friends at the burial service on February 25, 1837.

> The spirit of liberty appears to be looking out from its elevated throne with its pleasing mien and pointing to us, saying: "There are your brothers, Travis, Bowie, Crockett, and others whose valor places them in the rank of my heroes."

Despite the good will brought about during their common struggle, Juan Seguín and other Tejanos soon found that their Texian friends had short memories, and that they were the subjects of discrimination because of their Mexican background. Ultimately many of them went to Mexico to live, while others steeled themselves to withstand the insults of the *norteamericanos*. Texas made

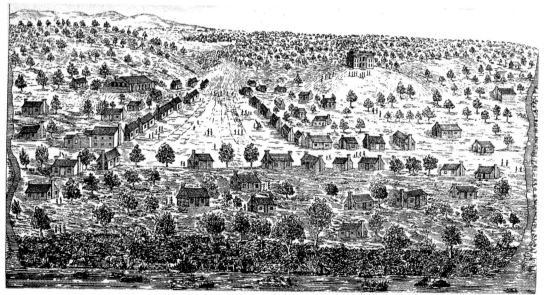

A VIEW OF THE CITY OF AUSTIN IN THE 1840S, LOOKING NORTH ACROSS THE COLORADO RIVER. PRESIDENT LAMAR'S HOUSE IS ON THE RIGHT AT THE TOP OF THE HILL. THE TEMPORARY CAPITOL IS THE LARGE BUILDING AT THE TOP LEFT. *TEXAS STATE LIBRARY & ARCHIVES COMMISSION*

Engraving of the Alamo monument, an elongated pyramidal stone structure with relief on four sides. Sculpted in 1841 by William B. Nangle, it was destroyed by fire in 1881. Fragments of the monument still exist.

Texas State Library & Archives Commission

THIS ETCHING OF THE FRONT OF THE ALAMO CHAPEL WAS CREATED AFTER THE 1850S, WHEN THE CHURCH WAS GIVEN ITS FAMOUS BELL-SHAPED PARAPET. *TEXAS STATE LIBRARY & ARCHIVES COMMISSION*

her lonely way in a cold world until the American desire for expansion to the Pacific and the possibility of English intrusion into the affairs of Texas at last brought about annexation and war with Mexico.

Today, at long last, the relations between Texians and Tejanos have improved, and there is a growing respect for the role that the Mexican-born Tejanos played in the liberation of Texas from Santa Anna's yoke. And the Alamo remains as it has been since 1836, a symbol of Texas independence and a monument to freedom for the world.

De la Peña's Diary at Auction

On November 18, 1998, the diary of José Enrique de la Peña was bought at auction in Los Angeles for $350,000 by two unidentified Texans. It had been held for many years with other de la Peña papers by the heirs of John Peace, a San Antonio lawyer and chairman of the University of Texas Board of Regents.

The papers have not all been translated from the Spanish, but the diary was translated in 1975 and immediately aroused a controversy that still rages: Did Davy Crockett die fighting in the plaza of the Alamo, swinging his rifle "Old Betsy" like a baseball bat, or did he try to surrender, only to be executed with six others by the direct order of General Santa Anna? This is the contention of the diary, a memoir said to have been kept by de la Peña in the 1830s.

Some Alamo historians have authenticated the diary while others have branded it as a work of fiction.

Peace bought the diary and other papers in the 1970s from the widow of a Mexican antique dealer. He and his heirs held the papers as part of the John Peace Collection at the library of the University of Texas at San Antonio, but in 1998 the heirs became worried by rumors that the University was about to break up the collection. They decided to put the de la Peña papers on the auction block. Another reason for the sale was that John Peace III was growing increasingly weary of answering questions about the authenticity of the diary.

Historians hoped that the purchasers would maintain the availability of the papers for researchers. Some scholars have expressed interest in translating more of the papers in hope of resolving the controversy over the manner of Davy Crockett's death.

Bibliography

Almonte, Juan Nepomuceno. "The Private Journal of Juan Nepomuceno Almonte, February 1–April 16, 1836." *Southwestern Historical Quarterly* 48 (July 1944).

Breihan, Carl W. "The True Story of the Alamo." *Denver Westerners Roundup* XIV (May 1958).

Chabot, Frederick C. *The Alamo: Mission, Fortress, and Shrine.* Privately Printed, 1936.

Chemerka, William R. *Alamo Almanac & Book of Lists.* Austin, TX: Eakin Press, 1986.

De Bruhl, Marshall. *Sword of San Jacinto: A Life of Sam Houston.* New York: Random House, 1994.

De la Peña, José Enrique. Edited and translated by Carmen Perry. *With Santa Anna in Texas.* College Station, TX: Texas A&M University Press, 1975.

Fehrenbach, T. R. *Lone Star: A History of Texas and Texans.* New York: Macmillan, 1968.

Hardin, Stephen L. *Texian Iliad.* Austin, TX: University of Texas Press, 1994.

Haythornthwaite, Philip. *The Alamo and Texan Independence, 1835–36.* London: Osprey, 1986.

Jackson, Ron. *Alamo Legacy.* Austin, TX: Eakin Press, 1997.

Long, Jeff. *Duel of Eagles.* New York: William Morrow, 1990.

Lord, Walter. *A Time to Stand.* Lincoln, NE: University of Nebraska Press, 1978.

Matovina, Timothy. *The Alamo Remembered: Tejano Accounts and Perspectives.* Austin, TX: University of Texas Press, 1995.

McAlister, George A. *Alamo: The Price of Freedom, A History of Texas.* Big Spring, TX: Docutex, 1990.

Myers, John. *The Alamo.* New York: E. P. Dutton, 1948.

Nofi, Albert A. *The Alamo and the Texas War for Independence.* New York: Da Capo Press, 1993.

Seguín, Juan (John). *The Personal Memoirs of John N. Seguin, 1834–1842.* San Antonio: Ledger Book and Job Office, 1858.

Todish, Tim J., and Terry S. Todish. *Alamo Sourcebook 1836.* Austin, TX: Eakin Press, 1998.

Tolliver, Ruby C. *Santa Anna: Patriot or Scoundrel.* Dallas, TX: Hendrick-Long, 1993.

Zavala, Lorenzo de. Edited and translated by Wallace Woolsey. *Journey to the United States of North America.* Austin, TX: Shoal Creek Publishers, 1980.

Index

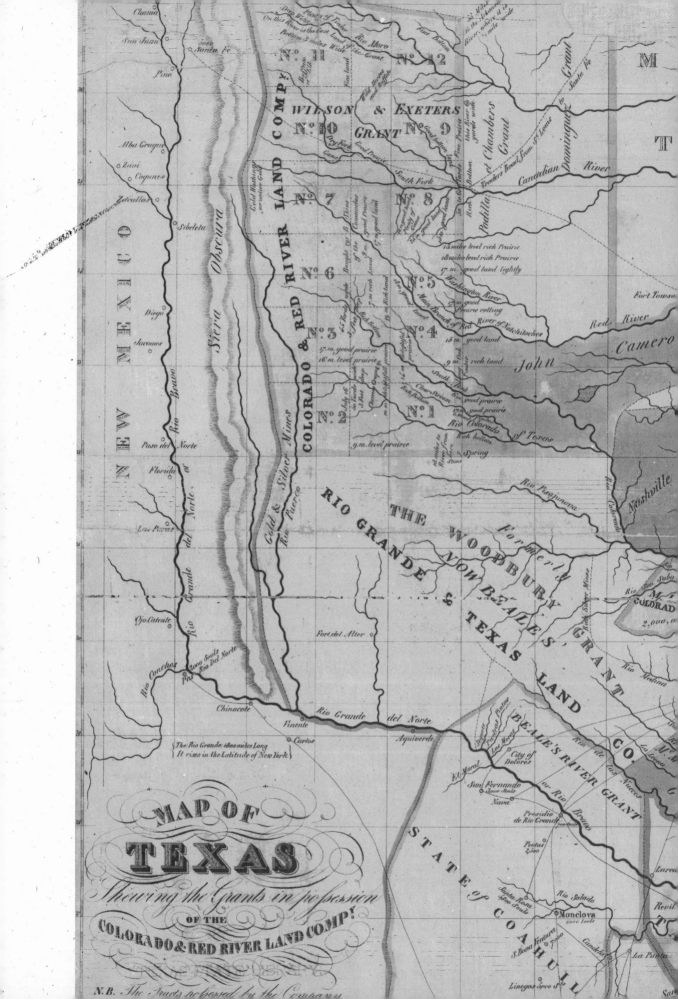